Inspired Drama Teaching

A companion website to accompany this book is available online at: http://education.west2.continuumbooks.com

Please type in the URL above and receive your unique password for access to the book's online resources.

If you experience any problems accessing the resources, please contact Continuum at: info@continuumbooks.com

Also available from Continuum

100 Ideas for Teaching Drama, Johnnie Young
Inspired English Teaching, Keith West
School Improvement Through Drama, Patrice Baldwin

INSPIRED DRAMA TEACHING

A Practical Guide for Teachers

Keith West

ANDOVER COLLEGE

continuum

Continuum International Publishing Group

The Tower Building	80 Maiden Lane
11 York Road	Suite 704
London	New York
SE1 7NX	NY 10038

www.continuumbooks.com

British Library Cataloguing-in-Publication Data
A catalogue record for this book is available from the British Library.
ISBN: 978-1-4411-5581-8 (paperback)

Library of Congress Cataloging-in-Publication Data
West, Keith, 1950–
  Inspired drama teaching : a practical guide for teachers / Keith West.
    p. cm. Includes index.
  ISBN 978-1-4411-5581-8
1. Drama—Study and teaching (Secondary). 2. Drama in education.
I. Title.

PN1701.W47 2011
792.071–dc22

                                                           2011008054

Typeset by Newgen Imaging Systems Pvt Ltd, Chennai, India
Printed and bound in India

Contents

Acknowledgements

This book is dedicated to all the students that I've had the pleasure of teaching and especially to the drama group from Ullswater High School, who casted me as 'Scrooge' in the short play we performed for their parents.

Many thanks to my wife, Ruth, and my son, Jonathan, who both slaved away for many hours editing this book. I am also indebted to Tim and Becka Coleman for their invaluable advice. Last but not least, my thanks also to Melanie Wilson from *Continuum* for her fantastic help, advice and support.

Keith West

CHAPTER 1

Why drama is important: a defence of the subject

When I first taught drama, years ago, the head teacher of the school I taught in mentioned to the head of English that the student teacher at the school was a very good drama teacher. He went on to say that when a certain particular student teacher taught drama there was no noise! The inference was that when I taught drama my students created noise and noise was a bad thing. There is, in my opinion, nothing wrong with noise provided that the noise is directed and on task! How can drama be taught without noise?

At that particular school, drama was taught in the hall, which was adjacent to the head teacher's study and the secretary's office. Drama was perceived as 'an English department thing' and undervalued. The head teacher demanded a high-quality school play each year, which he perceived as the school flagship. The play, in his opinion, was real drama and the only drama within the school that was worth having. How did he expect the performers to become expert drama students when he did not perceive drama as worth having lower down the school?

We've come a long way since then. Or have we? Even in the twenty-first century there are some schools that do not have drama departments and drama, if it happens at all, is either perceived as 'an English department thing' or an individual teacher's hobby horse!

In contrast to my experience at my first school, I taught at a very forward-looking school in Hampshire in the mid-1980s. At this school, the head teacher and senior management valued drama as a way of promoting learning across the curriculum. The drama department held a high status within the school and boasted its own large, purpose-built drama room. There was (luxury) a props room, a costume cupboard and plenty of technical apparatus. I was encouraged to participate in a nationwide oracy project and given time away from my normal timetable to work with other departments, thus ensuring that drama activities as a learning tool would work in subjects such as science, mathematics and art. During one memorable inset, the head teacher showed his staff a placard. It read;

Tell me and I will forget,
Show me and I will remember,
Involve me and I will understand.

The above words are not that head teacher's words. They are the words of the Greek philosopher, Aristotle.

It saddens me that many drama teachers still feel they need to justify their existence. Teachers from other subjects (and sometimes parents) fail to understand that learning takes place within the drama classroom.

Drama, if taught correctly, can stimulate creativity in problem solving across the curriculum. It can also challenge students' perceptions about themselves and about the world around them. Exploring ideas in drama can provide students with an outlet for their thoughts and emotions – which is important in a world of constant change. Many students today do not have a stable family unit. Many students live under quite challenging circumstances and have little outlet for their thoughts and emotions. For many in today's world, childhood is not a good place to be. Drama offers a release which, if kept bottled up, can cause problems within school and in the outside world.

Drama allows students to explore new ideas and experiment with personal choices and offers the opportunity to explore problem solving. Characters in real life and in fiction, face moral choices. The exploration of those choices is undertaken in a safe environment. Here, actions and consequences can be examined, discussed and experienced without the dangers and pitfalls that this type of experimentation would lead to in a real-life situation.

In today's world, despite all the work that has been achieved concerning oracy within the classroom, students' oral skills have declined. This is partly due to students spending so much time on their own – playing games on the computer or watching television, or listening to music. Participating in games in the street appears to be a thing of the past.

Drama promotes communication and it provides training in the practical aspects of communication. If drama is taught correctly, the activities that students engage with provide them with the confidence to speak in public. This type of work should translate into student confidence in both written and oral communication. Students should also be better placed to put themselves into 'other's shoes'. The benefits include the ability to relate to people from other social backgrounds and other age groups. Students should gain a more positive, confident self-image.

If taught correctly – dramatic activities encourage and promote self-control and discipline, which has its benefits across the curriculum. Students need to co-operate and work together in close collaboration during many drama activities. They have to listen and accept other students' points of view – which may radically differ from their own. Drama is essentially a collaborative exercise and it relates to the real world more than most subjects.

Drama promotes active learning, which should lead to a greater depth of understanding and an improvement in a student's ability to retain ideas and information.

I return to the obvious – people (adults and young people) learn best when they are enjoying their work. I do, don't you? Drama presents students with the opportunity to learn through practical and enjoyable work.

Creativity in approach

Drama, by its very nature, allows creativity in approach. Aristotle's line 'involve me and I will understand' is so apt here. A teacher talking about a subject or presenting a series of facts is unlikely to receive an enthusiastic response. I recall teaching a passage of Shakespeare and the AS students told me by their body language that they were bored. I placed them into groups and asked them to act out a scene each. Then we put the act together and they understood the work. What is more, they understood for the rest of the course! Because they had acted out a scene each, they had remembered and understood the whole act. A learning curve for me!

What can be done for an English play can be achieved across the curriculum. For example, in a history lesson, a scene from the First World War can be recreated within the classroom. Take trench life . . . a sentry on duty in the uniform of the times, sandbags and the teacher reading out a Sassoon or Wilfred Owen poem to evoke the right atmosphere. This could be followed by a factual account read and discussed. Students can then look at alternative viewpoints of the war (the English point of view or the German point of view) – all this would bring the lesson to life. For extra impact, the re-enactment of a shell attack, gas and soldiers dying would offer the opportunity for the students to write an 'eye witness' account of the events. Perhaps a small reading from Pat Barker's novel 'Regeneration' would add to the students' understanding of life in the trenches. I will explore cross-curricular opportunities and potential in a later chapter.

Why teach drama?

There are so many benefits for your students. The importance of drama lies in the nature of the learning experience it affords the student. Drama aids the development of key skills such as the imaginative enjoyment of the student's intellectual, emotional and physical capacities. This enables each student to embrace new perceptions and new understanding. Of course, drama aids concentration, confidence and co-operation right across the curriculum.

The benefits of drama go far beyond the drama classroom and even beyond school life, as the subject develops imagination and empathy.

Students develop the skills to understand other viewpoints, to develop and sustain arguments and to view situations from a variety of perspectives. For example, there might be a script concerning a parent's attitude towards their son's desire to meet up with his dubious friends. He is a shy boy who wants to be one of the crowd. He feels that hanging around town late at night will give him that acceptance. They are convinced the 'friends' will lead him into trouble. Both viewpoints are valid and can be fully explored within the drama room environment.

Although drama, because it is mostly a practical subject, can aid the kinaesthetic student, it can also help the visual and auditory student. Exploring and developing ideas requires intellectual and academic powers.

Due to its very nature and unique learning experience, drama is relevant to students with special educational needs. Drama can be of great benefit in aiding students who have language difficulties by extending their range of vocabulary and their ability to express emotions.

The physical aspect of drama will assist a student's non-verbal expression. Elements such as place, time and perceptions of relationships are cultivated through drama. A student's special awareness is also developed.

One aspect of drama is the story base and this will certainly aid the student's ability to understand the sequential nature of events.

Drama is a co-operative activity. It allows demanding students to understand the effect of their behaviour on other students. It also provides a valuable experience in working with others in order to achieve specific goals. Drama activities allow students to value the importance of taking turns and listening to others. Drama allows students to develop their key skills in areas such as communication, working with others and problem solving.

Another important aspect of drama is the opportunity to explore choice and the consequences of choice. It also explores the nature and types of conflict and the effect of conflict on others. It gives the opportunity for self-expression and self-realization.

Drama, therefore, is essential for a student's development.

Creativity in problem solving

By developing the imagination and the ability to see things in more than one way, students are able to problem solve across the curriculum. One co-operative piece of work is to ask students to imagine that the drama studio (or classroom) is a river they need to cross. The river runs from one side of the room to the other. The students are split into small groups of about five. They are each given four foam blocks (representing wooden blocks), two wooden planks (or something representing the planks) and a piece of rope. Their object is to cross the river without falling in. Make sure the planks are short, so that they can't reach the other side without using the blocks and the rope and some ingenuity. Observe how they co-operate as a team! A good team will use the planks to walk along, the blocks to use as stepping stones and the rope to tie themselves together. Or the first to cross might use the rope to aid weaker members of the team . . . so the weakest get across and the team score more points.

Creativity in problem solving can be used to study a play or a situation in a play, to explore the meaning behind a character's actions in a given situation or in deciding (in Science) which site is best for building a new industrial complex.

Challenging perceptions

Students are given the scope to challenge perceptions in drama. This should make them more reasonable and perceptive citizens. For example, the notion that all old people are senile and have nothing to contribute to society can be explored . . . noting that some notable British Prime Ministers have formed a government after the age of sixty-five. The idea that the state should do everything for you is another notion worth exploring . . . bringing in the J. F. Kennedy quote that you should ask not what your country has done for you but rather what you can do for your country. On a simpler level, you could explore the idea that school is boring and dull and has nothing to offer by allowing students to discover all that school does have to offer.

Communication

The importance of communication is explored through drama. As I pointed out in another book (*Inspired English Teaching*), 80% of our face to face communication is carried out non-verbally. Students are able to explore and imitate mannerisms – such as peoples' gestures and habits – the way people walk and act; how people look when they are frightened, disgusted or angry. Also, the way boys stand when talking to a girl they really like. Therefore; posture and hand signals are explored through drama as much as the spoken word. Characters can communicate through the *way* they dress, speak and walk as much as by *what* is spoken.

There are particular forms of communication used when an actor conveys subtle information to the audience. These will be explored through drama. These are;

- Eye contact. Your students will need to think about when and why they need to have (or avoid) eye contact with another actor or with an audience. When acting as a narrator, actors usually make eye contact with different audience members rather than looking into the far distance. It is not a good idea for an actor to focus on one person.

Role play (1)

Role play is beneficial to students in that it allows them to build up and develop a character. Ideally, role play should occur in a purpose-built drama studio. I appreciate, in individual schools, this may not be possible.

Before you begin role play with your students, you need to ask yourself what you want your students to get out of the experience. Unclear planning and preparation will result in unclear outcomes. The briefs you give your students should be clear and unambiguous. Are you assessing or developing skills? I suggest you develop skills through role play. Any hint of any type of assessment may make them nervous and they will underperform.

Role play can become ineffective if your students themselves are unclear in what they need to do – so do model an example.

A good introduction to role play is 'Giving Witness'. Pre-arrange with a student to run to your desk, take something from the desk (perhaps a bag) and run outside. This is more effective if you can use a student from another class. Ask two or three students to give an eye witness account of what happened. They need to describe the event they have just witnessed from their point of view.

Now show your students a clip from a film or an excerpt from the news. Perhaps there is a car chase that ends in an accident, or a robbery caught on CCTV. Allow two or three students to give the account from their point of view.

Finally, ask them to role play a police interview concerning an eye-witness account of a crime. They can take it in turns to be the police officer and the eye witness.

Another idea I have used with success is the secret role play. Ask students to work in pairs, then ask one of them to take a piece of paper. The paper will have either A or B printed on it. If the student who picks the paper is A, the other must be B. A has one set of instructions and B has another. A (the parent) is anxious to know how B got on at school. B does not want to mention that (s)he was wrongfully accused of stealing. If the pair fail to develop their role play, intervene as C, a friend who unfortunately mentions part of the incident in front of the parent!

Depending upon the age of the students, you might like to consider some of the following role-play possibilities.

- Telling secrets.
- An interview situation.
- An argument (this must go somewhere).
- A film star meets a producer.
- A footballer meets a fan.
- A vegetarian talks to a meat eater.

Here are some examples of student role play, '*Telling Secrets*' was written and performed by Jade Bland and Mel Bostock, Year 7.

Jade: Bet you wanna know all my little secrets, don't you?

Mel: (*surprised*) Go on!

Jade: I poisoned my grandma's cat.

Mel: (*shocked*) You did!

Jade: (*upset*) Didn't mean to. I was only young. It happened six years ago. I was staying in her big house in Suffolk.

Mel: And?

Jade: Grandma told me to feed the big ginger thing. The cat was a really large tom.

Mel: (*interested*) So?

Jade: (*thoughtful*) I knew the cat food was in Gran's cupboard. I put the food into the tom's bowl and noticed some white powder. I didn't realise the powder was rat poison.

Mel (*surprised*) Couldn't you read or something?

Jade: (*defensive*) No, not then (*pause*) Anyway . . . I sprinkled the powder on top of the food. I thought I was doing the cat a favour. The powder looked like the stuff mum sprinkled on top of cup cakes. Then I thought Gran might be angry, so I mixed it all up.

Mel: So what happened?

Jade: (*softly*) The cat died. (*head bowed*) I've felt guilty ever since. Gran still misses that ginger tom, she's never had another cat since.

Mel: (*sympathetic*) You were young then, you couldn't be held responsible.

Jade: (*whispering*) You're the first person I've ever told.

Mel (*low*) Well, I have a secret . . . it is more terrible than yours . . . you won't like me when I've finished telling it! My secret is so bad, so wicked, you'll never think of me as the same person . . . ever again!

Your students might wish to role play that activity and then improvise and role play Mel's secret.

A footballer meeting a fan might have many possibilities. Ask your students to read the two short extracts. The first is by Allan Merrion and Sean Wood (Year 8).

A Footballer Meets A Fan

Sean: (*waving the team scarf*) Fantastic! Allan Merrion! I'm actually face to face with Allan Merrion.

Allan: (*bored*) Yeah, whatever!

Sean: (*enthusiastic*) Awesome goal you scored against United last week. Must be the goal of the season . . . what a striker, what a finisher!

Allan: (*showing interest*) You saw that goal, the one I booted in with my left foot?

Sean: (*over the top*) Saw? I was there, I was there! With me mates, on the terraces. Amazing! Awesome! Fan-tastic! What a goal! A thunder-shot. Keeper had no chance.

Allan: (*shrugs his shoulders*) You didn't think it was . . . just a tad offside?

Sean: (*laughs*) Offside! No way! From where *I* was standing it was onside. Awesome!

Allan: (*warming to Sean*) Did you see the two I scored against City last month?

Sean: See them? I was there, mate. One a clear header and the other . . . pure poetry. You dribbled past three defenders . . . dummied . . . shot. Beat the keeper . . . he went the wrong way. Pure magic, genius!

Allan: Pity we lost those matches. Pity we're relegated.

Working in pairs, your students may wish to role play a meeting between the manager and Allan. The manager is not pleased that the team are relegated and thinks Allan should have scored more goals.

Two of my Year 8 students had a different 'take' on the meeting between a footballer and a fan.

A Footballer Meets A Fan (2) by Sanja Raj and Felicity Stocker (Year 8)

Sanja: (*to the footballer*) What a load of rubbish. My gran could've played better.

Steve: (*sneers*) Yeah and what I need right now is friendly fire, right?

Sanja: (*annoyed*) I pay good money to see you waste great chances. There were golden opportunities to score – and you couldn't convert any!

Steve: (*still sneering*) I'd like to see you do any better.

Sanja: (*explaining*) That isn't the point. The point is, you're paid to score goals. I'm paid to deliver the post.

Your students might like to develop this piece of role play.

Self-image and exploring together

Drama is a useful tool for working on a student's self-image. By group co-operation and inspiring drama games and exploring life through other peoples' shoes, a student can experiment and 'become' a different person. The shy student can gain confidence through games and through role play.

Considering classroom management

An ideal drama environment is a purpose-built drama studio with enough room to place desks and chairs in a particular area, possibly to one side of the room.

Drama is a subject that allows imagination and free expression. There needs to be enough space to allow the students a controlled freedom of movement. In other words, they need an area that is free from desks and chairs. Ideally, desks and chairs need to be nearby for certain collaborative activities such as script writing. Having mentioned the above, I have taught drama in school halls and classrooms as well as school-designed drama studios.

Whatever the working environment, as a drama teacher you will need to put in place clear structures. This is due to the fact that many students initially see drama as a game without rules . . . an easy option. However, actors are people who work hard to achieve a false sense that their part in a play, film or television series is easy. It isn't! Most actors (if not all) are disciplined and focused. In other words, they work very hard to achieve an illusion of normality.

As a drama teacher, you need to set up a list of rules, aims and objectives. Here are some that worked for me. (Remember, the drama room is your domain. It reflects your personality. You want the students to perceive your classroom as a safe, calm place where learning will happen.)

Keep the drama room interesting and clean. Do not allow the classroom to be strewn with sweet wrappers and make sure there are no blobs of chewing gum stuck on the seats or in the dark corners of the drama room. Somehow, students initially understand drama to be a place where indiscipline happens. You can change this perception by creating order. As mentioned in my book *Inspired English Teaching* (page 13) I used to carry a tin of cleaning powder and a cloth into my classrooms. If I caught a student writing on a desk, I would ask the student to clear up the mess. When a class was ready to leave the room, I used to check that all was in order. I made sure the room was litter and graffiti free. If I did spot any mess, I'd politely ask if the room could be in the same state as it was when the class entered the room. They soon got the message! A drama room is no less important than any other classroom. An ordered clean drama room, with any props carefully put away, sends a clear message to every student.

Displays

An interesting and frequent turn-over of displays is important. It shows students that you take an interest in the state of the room.

Some displays can be pictures of famous actors or they can be of a Shakespearian or local production. Perhaps some displays could be of any written work achieved in drama or photographs of students working on a drama piece.

Displays should be interesting to look at. It is important to make sure there is a quick turnover of display. Old displays that are faded and peeling off the walls are actually, in my experience, counterproductive and act as a disincentive to students.

If at all possible, keep the displays connected to the current learning that is taking place in the drama room.

Standards of work

Make sure you quickly establish your way of working. Make clear and understandable expectations as to how you expect the students will behave. Below are bullet points indicating what I did when teaching drama – please feel free to use or adapt as appropriate.

- I made the students line up outside the drama room and asked them to file past me and sit in an appropriate chair.
- I insisted that bags and coats be placed beside the chairs they were sitting on or placed in the far corner of the room.
- I asked the students to form a circle, sitting on the floor.
- I stood in the middle of the circle and told them what to expect . . . which was as follows;
  1. A clap of my hands meant an activity could start.
  2. A loud and continuous clap of my hands meant students were required to stop doing their activity . . . immediately. Those that carried on were sent to the seating area and had to observe the activity. Persistent offenders were required

to make up time lost during a lunch break or after school. With some groups, I showed them a red card, giving the clear indication that I had the type of authority invested in a referee of a football match. A red card means time out and a school detention.

3. I insisted on silence when another student talked to the group. I pointed out the importance of listening skills, which are crucial to drama.

CHAPTER 2

Exploring drama

Ice breakers

Ice breakers are an excellent way of getting new students into drama. There are so many possible ice-breaker activities and some of these are very well known. I am going to mention those that I have trialled and tested, that have worked for me. Some of these are well known and will be familiar to experienced drama teachers and some are not so well known.

What are ice breakers?

Ice breakers can be used when you are new to a group or there is a new student member of the group. They are also useful as starter exercises when the group members are shy with each other.

How do ice breakers work?

They help a new group of students get to know each other. They can help a new student integrate into a group. They can encourage students to work together and they allow social skills to develop.

What's my name?

For a new group, this is an excellent game. It allows students to quickly get to know each other's names. It is also a very good way for the drama teacher to quickly get to know all the students' names! If, like me, you struggle with student names, this game will be like a lifeline for a drowning sailor. Knowing a student's name also improves discipline. It is better to say, 'What are you doing, Jake? It would be great if you could join the others on this task,' than 'You over there . . . ' The 'you over there . . . ' disturbs everyone. If Jake is so inclined, he will play ignorant. If his name is called, it is much more effective. Others can carry on with their task and Jake has no excuses. Incidentally, if you do not know a student's name and you want to attract his attention, try non-verbal signals such as catching his eye and shaking your head or beckoning him to you.

For the game of 'What's my name?' you will need a softball or a bean bag. You then ask the group to stand in a wide circle – assuming that you have enough space to allow this! You throw the softball towards a student and call out the student's name. All students need to concentrate and keep their eye on the ball. The student who catches the ball becomes the thrower, the thrower must say their name and the name of the person they are throwing to. For example;

> 'Janice to Matt.'
> 'Matt to Jez.'
> 'Jez to Cindy.'
> And so on . . .

If you have the space, the softball can be thrown quickly. If the catcher fails to catch the ball, they are out! (You need to judge if the throw was fair; if not the thrower is out. Your judgement is final and any dissenters are shown a red card.) This game could continue until there are only two participants left in. The remaining two are given a small reward . . . perhaps a school merit. Don't be slavish though; if you feel the students sitting out are becoming restless, kill the game and go on to another activity.

The game show

This is another way for you to learn names. Ask your students to sit in a circle and imagine they are hosts of a game show. Nod at one of the students, who stands up and introduces himself to the group – saying two things about himself. He then introduces somebody else in the group. If he does not know that person's name, he will need to point. For example;

> Hi, I'm Lisa and I have two pet rabbits. I also enjoy exercising my friend's pony. Here is Terry.

> Hi, I'm Terry. I love playing football and I support Colchester United. Let me introduce you to the one and only Angela Brooks.

A name game

This is another game that can be used with an unfamiliar group. Place them in a circle and ask each student to step forward and do something that reflects their personality. For example, Suzanne might run into the middle of the circle and do a diving pose, indicating that she is the local diving champion and a good swimmer. As she strikes her pose, she should shout out her name. The other students must stand and copy Suzanne, shouting out her name.

Wink/murder

This is a very well-known and successful drama game. If you don't know it, this game is certainly worth trying with your students.

Ask your students to sit in a circle and close their eyes. Walk around the group and tap one student lightly on the shoulder. That student becomes the detective and will come to the centre of the circle. Tap another student twice on the shoulder. That student remains sitting in the circle but is the murderer.

The object of the game is for the murderer to wink at as many people as possible before the detective catches the murderer. The detective is allowed three guesses.

As a variation, you can have two detectives. When you know the group well and discipline is not an issue, the victims can 'die' in an interesting way. I have allowed students to clutch their throats or twitch or scream as they slowly die.

The sandwich memory game

Ask your students to sit in a circle. You say, 'We are going to make a big sandwich and in it I put a layer of cream cheese.' You then call out a student's name. Rory will continue the game by saying, 'In the sandwich I put a layer of cream cheese and two sardines.' He then calls Sarah's name. Sarah will continue by saying, 'In the sandwich I put a layer of cream cheese, two sardines and a lettuce leaf.' . . . and so on!

The game is played until a student forgets the sequence. This activity allows the students to build up their memory skills.

As a variation, you could say, 'We are going to make a revolting sandwich and in it I put a squashed frog,' and so on!

Items from a bag

Ask your students to sit in a circle. You have a large bag in your hand. You take five items from the bag, which you have pre-selected. You ask some students what they could use the items for. They must use their imaginations. However, each student must give his/her name before a guess (idea) is allowed.

Example: Take a comb from the bag, a shell from the beach, a short stick, a screwdriver and a magnifying glass.

Student A could say; 'My name's Amanda and I think the comb could be used to search for fleas in an old dog.' Student B could say, 'I'm called Jake and I'd use a magnifying glass to start a fire if I was lost in the jungle.' Student C could say, 'They call me Hopper but my real name's Simon. I think the shell gives me the sound of the sea, if it's next to my ear.'

You may need to give students the above examples to get them thinking. When they have got the right idea, you take the students that have contributed from the circle – in the example, Amanda, Jake and Simon would be taken out. You select students for them and ask them to create a quick improvisation from their ideas. Amanda's group would search for fleas in an old dog. One of the group would become the old flea-ridden dog!

'Whozon'

In this ice breaker, one student is chosen to be the searcher. After the searcher leaves the room, another student is chosen to be the 'whozon'. The 'whozon' makes actions that change about every thirty seconds or so. 'Whozon' might clap their hands, scratch their ear, shake their head, nod. The rest of the group quickly imitate 'whozon'. The searcher enters the room and has to work out who is the 'whozon'. The searcher is allowed three guesses. The 'whozon' needs to constantly change actions without getting caught.

For any student who is deliberately looking at the 'whozon' or nodding in the general direction of the 'whozon', to give the game away and aid the searcher, is given a red card and has to sit out the next round. As most students enjoy the game, the red card is definitely seen as a punishment.

The hello game

Allow your students to walk around the drama room. When you clap your hands, they must freeze and then say hello to the nearest person. The aim of the game is to offer a new way to greet somebody on each occasion. You keep control by telling them who they are saying hello to. For example;

- Say hello to your best friend.
- Say hello to your grandparent.
- Say hello to a famous person.
- Say hello to an alien.
- Say hello to somebody you dislike.
- Say hello to somebody you admire.
- Say hello to your teacher.
- Say hello to a long lost friend.

The students take it in turns to greet the other person. Keep the activity moving fast, so that the students need to think quickly.

Copy walk

Ask the group to work in pairs. The pair choose to be A or B. Ask A to walk around the room. B observes for about ten seconds before following and copying A. After a lap around the room, B becomes the walker. After a further lap, ask A to walk in a silly or exaggerated way. B has to copy. Then ask B to walk with a limp, A has to do the same.

Copy walk is good for concentration and observation skills. Most students enjoy this activity but the trick is to keep it moving fast. For a reluctant or special educational needs group, do not be afraid to model the activity first.

Rabbit and fox

This activity works best in a hall or drama room and not so well in a conventional classroom.

However . . .

This is what you need to do;

1) Divide your class into two equal teams.
2) Line them up at one side of the room with a gap of about two metres between the teams.
3) Ask your two groups to face each other. Each student should now be opposite the other. The teams need to be divided equally.
4) Call one team 'rabbits' and the other team 'foxes'.
5) Explain that foxes must tag the rabbits before they reach the safety of the back wall.
6) Call for silence. Make sure the two-metre gap exists between the two teams. Then shout 'rabbits'. The foxes have to catch the rabbits before they reach the far wall.

(The foxes have a chance to catch the rabbits, as the rabbits need to turn round before they can run!)

- Once at the other side of the room, the two teams can line up again and the foxes become rabbits, the rabbits become foxes.
- To confuse the students after a few rounds, shout 'rodents'. See how many still run!

Accept no nonsense. Any cheating is 'rewarded' by a red card and the student will sit out the remainder of the game. Keep the activity moving fast and don't go beyond about four or five rounds.

For a quick ice breaker, try '**The interview**'. Divide the group into pairs. A is then to interview B for up to three minutes. Each interviewer has to discover three interesting facts about their partner. Bring everyone back together and ask them to present the facts about their partner to the rest of the group. Then B interviews A and presents the facts to the rest of the group.

For example: Chloe about Briony–

> I discovered three interesting facts about Briony. She is an auntie – her older sister had a baby boy called Joe. She visited Denmark last year and she's seen Copenhagen. She almost died just after her birth.

Jeff about Chuck.

> Three facts about Chuck, he's English but he has an American mother. He has climbed Ben Nevis in Scotland with an outward bound group and . . . now this is unusual . . . Ben and his twin have invented their own language.

This activity improves students' memory skills as they have to remember and recall three facts about their partner.

Truth or lies

Ask your students to write three pieces of information about themselves which may not be known by the rest of the group. Two of the pieces of information are correct and one is a lie. In turn, students read the three pieces of information about themselves and the rest of the group vote on which is true and which is a lie. The vote can be by a show of hands. The group (in my experience) are often surprised. They usually believe the lie!

Example:

> **Achla**: I was born in India. I have two sisters and a brother and my dad owns the 'Taste of India' restaurant in town.
> **Tim**: You don't have a brother.
> **Achla:** I do . . . he's in Year 7.
> **Simon**: You were born in Essex.
> **Achla:** True. My mum and dad were born in India.

This activity presents students with the chance of getting to know each other better. You do not need to keep students in one big circle for this activity. It moves along faster if you divide the group into three or four equal circles.

Talking and discussing

Give each student a piece of paper. The paper has a set of random questions they need to follow but in no particular order. The students have to find out the answers to each question.

This game is great for getting the group to mix and is also a game for starting conversations. Everyone *has* to speak to everyone else. Nobody can remain silent!

The set of questions you hand out could include the following;

- How many students have a sister?
- Who has the longest journey into school?
- What is the strangest thing anyone has eaten?
- Who has a pet cat?
- Who has a fear of flying?
- Who has been to New Zealand?
- Who has the strangest hobby?
- Who was born in this area?
- How many of you live in a house with five bedrooms?
- How many students have a great-grandparent still living?

Tip: Do not allow any student to shout out the question. They each need to ask individual students, not groups. Any student disobeying these instructions should be handed a red card and made to sit out this activity.

When most students have completed this activity, check if they are right by reading out the questions and asking for a show of hands for most of the questions. For these questions, ask a student for the answer they have and see who agrees.

Questions, questions

Ask your students to stand in a circle. Throw a soft ball or a bean bag gently at a student. When the student has caught the ball, (s)he has to answer one of the questions listed below, – which you have written on a flip chart or on an overhead screen.

When the question is answered, the student throws the ball to another member of the group, who answers a question from the list.

This activity helps students know more about each other. At the end of the game (which should last for no more than fifteen minutes) make sure you tell them that each of their contributions was of value.

Here are the twenty questions – but please do adapt according to the age and ability of your particular group.

1. If you had a time machine that would take you to a place in the past, where would you go to? Bear in mind that you cannot return!
2. You have won a competition to meet a famous person. Who would you meet and what might you say to them?
3. If your home was flooded, what three items would you want to save?
4. Imagine you were given £10,000 but you had to spend the money by the end of the day, what would you spend the money on?

5. If you were forced to give up one of your senses, which one would it be and why? (With some groups, it might be necessary to list the senses – hearing, seeing, feeling, smelling, tasting.)
6. If you could be changed into somebody else, who would you be and why?
7. Imagine you were given an extra gift or ability – which would it be? (Author note: For me, it would be the gift of singing in tune!)
8. What is your favourite season of the year? Why?
9. If you were changed into an animal, which would it be and why?
10. Who is your favourite soap opera character? Why?
11. If you had your life over again, what would you do differently?
12. If you could change something in the world, what would it be?
13. Imagine you were at a restaurant with somebody very important and you took a mouthful of something that tasted very bad, what would you do?
14. Is there a video or a film that you have seen recently that you would recommend? Why would you recommend it?
15. If you had to live in a different country, which one would you choose and why?
16. What pet would you like to own and why?
17. Imagine you were cast onto a desert island for a month, what five items would you take with you? Why?
18. If any one of your dreams could come true, which one would it be? Explain the dream.
19. Imagine you could learn a new skill – which skill would you choose?
20. Where would you like to be in ten years' time? What might you be doing?

Ape/rabbit /wizard

Ask your students to break into pairs. With a younger group, demonstrate what an ape (long arms, stern face) rabbit (long ears, twitching nose) and wizard (tall straight, holds wand) look like. Now explain that apes eat rabbits (ape wins) and rabbits run from wizards (rabbit wins) but wizards turn apes into stone (wizard wins). A and B quickly decide which of the three they will be and the best of three is the winner. This game is played like the scissors/rock/paper game. Eventually, a group champion emerges.

Opposites

In a circle, your students pass a soft ball to each other. They then have to try and catch or head the ball. You shout 'head the ball' or 'catch the ball'. At an appropriate time, you tell them that when you shout 'head the ball' they need to catch it! If you call 'catch the ball' they need to head it!

Tip: Play the game quickly and end it after a few rounds. The aim of the game is to aid concentration.

Line up

Give each student a number. The object of the game is to get the students to line up in numerical order as fast as possible. They need to do this by communicating to each other without speaking or holding up fingers. They usually achieve their goal by inventing a sign language of their own!

A variation: Make the activity competitive. Divide your group into two or three equal teams and see who achieves the required order first.

Make it harder: Ask the teams to arrange themselves by their birth month or by who is the tallest, going down to the shortest.

Fears

Ask your students to write a personal fear anonymously on a piece of paper. Collect the paper and ask each member of the group to select and read another student's fear to the group. The reader must then explain how the writer might feel about that particular fear.

This activity enhances interpersonal skills.

Possible fears. (For reluctant students you might suggest some of the following – although most students are not reluctant, because the fear is anonymous and remains so.)

1) Of being in a field with a bull.
2) Not able to make friends.
3) Growing old.
4) Flying in an aeroplane.
5) Failing all their exams.
6) Dogs.

Warm ups

Some students have difficulty 'suspending disbelief' at the start of a drama lesson. The transition from a lesson sitting down at a desk and the demands made by drama might appear daunting. Warm ups help students to quickly focus on drama. Warm ups prepare students for the forthcoming main activity or focus of the lesson. They get the students into a 'drama mood'. Warm ups, used at the start of a lesson, are effective. Some ice breakers can be used as warm ups but ideally, warm ups should use a student's body and voice. For a fidgety group, good warm-up exercises will get them going, help them to concentrate and help them focus on the work in hand. Experienced drama teachers may well know some of these activities. These are all games I have used – and found to be successful – over a number of years.

Use of space

1) Using the whole space available, ask your students to walk quickly around the space – using all the available space. Tell them to move in different directions and not in a circle. Tell them to walk quickly and briskly around the room as if they had a purpose . . . as if they were late for a lesson.
2) Tell them to walk slowly, like a very old or a sick person.
3) Tell them to walk around the space as if they were a king or a queen.
4) Ask them to walk around the room avoiding eye contact.
5) Now ask them to walk around the room making eye contact with other students.
6) Finally, ask them to imagine they are wading through a swamp, moving through the desert and then walking on thin ice.

This activity works well if you frequently change the movement. You can sometimes ask them to change direction, then change again. This keeps them focused.

The small fish game

If your students need something very energetic, get them to play the small fish game as a warm-up activity.

Tell your students to form a circle. They will need plenty of space, so the circle should be as large as possible. There should be space around the outside of the circle, though. Go around the back of the circle and name the 'fish'. The first can be 'cod', the second is 'squid', the third is 'haddock' and the final fish is 'small fry'. The fifth is 'cod', the sixth is 'squid' and so on – until each student is named. Shout out one of the fish names and all the 'fish' with that name need to run around the outside of the circle, clockwise. You step from the circle and into one of the spaces left by the named fish. The named fish then need to scramble for a space. One of the named fish will not find a space and will be out.

After a few rounds, place all the group back into the circle, then call out two fish group. For example, 'Cod, run clockwise, small fry run anti-clockwise'. You can tell them that when you clap your hands, the fish need to change direction. Then, step into a space.

Continue to play the game until one fish group has won.

The object of this exercise is for the students to let off steam, so they can concentrate better!

Suggestions: let's . . .

Ask a student to suggest an activity they can all mimic. The student might shout, 'Let's play tennis'. The group then quickly need to imitate playing tennis. After a short while, shout 'freeze' and another student might shout, 'Let's draw' and the students mimic drawing a picture.

Take up about five or six suggestions before moving on to a new activity. This exercise is a useful warm up for improvisation work.

Eye on the ball

Ask your students to form a circle. You need about five soft balls but use only one initially. Throw a ball gently at a student, who catches it. Then the student will need to throw the ball at somebody else in the circle. The ball is thrown around the circle and, as the game progresses, you can throw in a second ball. Then throw in a third and a fourth and possibly a fifth. Tell your students to keep the flow going. They will need to concentrate hard.

If a ball is not caught or dropped, start the game again – with just the one ball and build the game up as you did originally.

Any student throwing the ball in such a way that it is impossible to catch, is given a red card and has to sit out the activity.

This game forces students to concentrate and keep their focus.

Clap ball

Ask your students to stand in a circle. Throw a small ball towards a student. The student must catch the ball and nod to another student before the ball is thrown. Once a certain rhythm is established, ask your group to clap once the ball is in the air. If this works, see if they can clap twice while the ball is in the air . . . and so on until the ball is dropped!

As a variation, make the game a challenge. Split the group into two teams, forming two circles. See which group can clap the most while the ball is in the air!

This exercise aids focus and concentration. As a tip – make it clear to your students that the thrower has the responsibility as to whether the catcher can catch the ball. This should also be a golden rule for all catch and throw ball games in drama.

Piggy in the middle (two games)

Split your students into groups of three. One of the three steps into the middle. The middle place is C. A throws the ball to B and C has to intercept. When C has intercepted, the player that has failed to catch the ball goes into the middle.

Piggy in the middle (2)

Using the space, four students are chosen to stand in each corner of the room. A fifth student is chosen to stand in the middle. Two students at any of the corners try to swap places by nodding at each other and running. They need to move as quickly as possible before Piggy can get to the vacant corner.

Note: A student is not allowed to return to the corner they have just vacated. The object of the game is to see how long it takes for Piggy to remain as Piggy.

A variation of the game is to place Piggy in the middle and Piggy has to intercept a runner by tagging the runner.

Incidentally, I first came across this game as a football training exercise.

Outer and inner circle

Ask your students to form an outer and an inner circle of an equal number. The outer circle looks inwards, the inner circle looks out-wards. In other words, they face each other. Each student is looking at someone! Ask them to start a conversation. You might wish to offer some suggestions.

- What did you eat for lunch yesterday?
- What sport do you like watching/playing best?
- What did you do last weekend?
- What is your favourite film?
- What is your favourite T.V. programme?

(Please add as appropriate for your group.)

When you clap your hands the conversation starts, when you next clap your hands, the conversation stops and the inner circle moves once to the right, like a cog in a machine. Clap your hands and the conversation restarts – but each member of the group will be con-versing with a new student.

It is best to restrict this game to four or five conversations. Should you wish to develop this activity, you could ask some students to retell the best conversation they had during that time.

The rain game

Ask your students to sit in a circle. Rub the palms of your hands together, making a swishing sound. Ask everyone to join in. Once your students have imitated the swishing sound, begin to snap your fingers, in a rhythm, like falling rain. Your students should switch their actions, too. Next, slap your lap with the palms of your hands. This indicates that the rain is falling faster. When you want the storm to reach its peak, stamp your feet loudly. When your students are following your actions, calm the storm by doing the actions backwards, in sequence. As the storm diminishes, your actions can slow down . . . until you end in silence.

Extra activity

Ask a student to do everything you have done, in the correct sequence. The exercise aids group focus.

Word association

Ask your students to sit in a circle. Then ask one student to throw the soft ball gently at another. As the student throws the ball (s)he shouts out a word, for example 'bear'. The catcher might say 'polar', having associated bear with a type of bear. The next catcher might say 'ice' and the following catcher might say 'cream' and so on!

This exercise is good for focusing and thinking and listening skills.

Action changing

Ask your students to stand in a circle. The first student might do an action, such as pretending to fish. The second student guesses and says, 'you are fishing, what must I do?' The fishing student says, 'I want you to post a letter.' The second student 'posts a letter' and a third student says, 'You are posting a letter, what must I do?' The second student says, 'I want you to wash a car' and so on, until everyone in the circle has had the chance to ask a question, mime an action and present a student with an action to perform. For some students, you might need a flip chart with ideas listed. Here are just a few ideas–

1) Teach a class.
2) Play a game.
3) Write a letter.
4) Groom a pony.
5) Stroke a cat.
6) Walk a dog.

7) Chew gum.
8) Buy new clothes.
9) Try on new clothes.
10) Drive a car.

This is a further game for developing and aiding concentration.

Freeze and do

Ask your students to sit around your acting area, perhaps in a semi-circle. Two students improvise a scene. They are allowed to use dialogue and as much physical action as possible. When it becomes obvious as to what is happening in the improvised piece, any student can shout 'freeze'. The two actors must stop immediately and freeze the action. The student who stopped the scene is allowed to tap one of the actors on the shoulder and take the original actor's position. The actor then becomes part of the audience.

The new actor must now initiate a new scene, which has to be a new storyline. The new actor's responsibility is to communicate to the other actor what the scene is about, without telling that actor. The communication must be through action and speech.

For example:

New Actor: This is a terrible tragedy. It took part in her own home too.
   Whatever is the world coming to?
Old Actor: I'm not sure. I'm confused.
New Actor: A single shot to the head.
Old Actor: (understanding) Ah yes, but what was the motive?
New Actor: Money. It's always about money.

A student might have picked up that the storyline is about a murder and (s)he might shout 'freeze' and take over.

You can make a rule that every member of the group has to shout 'freeze' and take over once. It is up to the audience how long that person stays in the acting area.

The complete picture

Split your group into three or four, depending upon the size of your group. Each group has to create a picture. For example, one student shouts 'I'm a house,' and stands in the centre of the group. Another shouts, 'I'm the garden next to the house,' and takes his place next to 'the house'. Another shouts, 'I'm a bench in the garden' and sits down next to the garden. The next student shouts, 'I'm a cat sitting on the bench,' and that student sits near 'the bench'.

Thus, a 'picture' is created.

Use this with younger students and keep the action moving fast, so that they don't have time to think but act through word association.

Everyone who . . .

This is an all action warm-up game. Ask your students to sit on a chair in a circle. If you have time, pre-arrange the circle of chairs before the students arrive for your lesson. Make sure there is one less chair than there is a student. The student without a chair is 'It'. Ask 'It' to shout something out that might apply to some students but not to them all. For instance, the student might shout out 'All those who have a pet dog.' All the students who have a pet dog must move to a different chair. 'It' also needs to find a chair. The student without a chair becomes 'It'. The new 'It' might say, 'All those who are left handed.' Those who are left handed need to move! And so on . . .

Tip: As 'It' has to move, whatever 'It' shouts out has to apply to 'It'. For example, if 'It' shouts out 'All those who are left handed,' then 'It' has to be left handed!

Mother, mother

This is a game I've played with groups for years – I do not know where it came from.

Ask one student to stand in the middle of the room. The middle of the room represents the middle of a large river. Mother is like a river god. The student in the middle of the room is mother (or father). The others chant, 'Mother, mother, can I cross your golden water?' Mother, with her back turned makes up something that might apply to some but not to all. She might say, 'Only those who are wearing a watch.' Those who are wearing a watch are allowed across the river. Those not wearing a watch are chased by mother. Any caught are 'out'. Those who run across the 'river' to the other side without being tagged (caught) are still in. Last person caught is the next mother (or father).

This game is good for improving concentration.

Statues

This is another high-energy game. A student is chosen to stand at the far end of the room, facing the wall. That Student is Movement Spotter. The class creep forward. If the student turns round and spots anyone creeping forward, they need to return to base. The idea is for the students to watch Movement Spotter closely and creep forward without being noticed. When Movement Spotter begins to turn round, the students must freeze. At some point, some students will be near

Movement Spotter. They might attempt to run forward and touch him/
her. Once touched, Movement Spotter becomes a student and the one
who touched Movement Spotter is the new Movement Spotter.

This game is good for improving concentration.

Avoid eye contact

Ask your students to stand in a circle. They must all look at the
floor. You shout, 'Look Up.' They all have to look directly into the
face of someone else in the circle. Most of the students will be looking at somebody who is not looking at them. If they are catching
each other's stare, they must chant, 'Stare me out, stare me out' and
quickly change places with that other person.

Numbers game

Ask your students to walk around the room, using all the available
space. After a short while, shout out a number. All the students must
try and get into groups – making that exact number. Any groups or
individuals that fail to get into that number are out.

Tip: After a while, if you want to finish the game, shout out a
number greater than the students left in!

Improvisation

This is all about making it up as you go along. It is unplanned by the
students, although you can still direct the students by giving them a
storyline. Improvisation allows all the students in the group to take
part in the action.

1) The alphabet game

This is a good game to introduce students to the concept of improvisation. They are forced to think quickly. It is interesting to see how
far down the alphabet they can go before they come unstuck.

For the first try at the alphabet game, it is useful to give your
students a situation before they begin. Perhaps suggest getting into
trouble at school. This can take off in several different directions.

Ask your students to get into pairs. They then need to work
through the alphabet with one-line conversations. For example–

A: Anyone seen Annabelle?
B: Before you tell me where she is, I know she's in trouble.
A: Could be!
B: Don't tell me you don't know.
A: Everyone knows she's with the Head of Year.
B: Frightening!

A: (*sarcastic*) Great thinking of Annabelle, to nick a library book.
B: How did she steal the book? The library is like Fort Knox.
A: I don't know.
B: Janice will know, she was with Annabelle.

–And so on.

As a variation, ask your students to work in groups of three and go through the alphabet backwards, starting at Z and ending at A.

In the library

This exercise is useful in getting your students to think quickly. In groups of three or four, ask your students to improvise a short scene in the library. They are all sitting down at the same table (they could improvise this if necessary). They need to talk about something, rather than acting out a murder or a fight. For example;

A: What did you do last night?
B: Went to the fair.
C: Didn't know the fair had arrived yet.
D: You lot, I need to borrow someone's homework.
B: (*ignoring D*) The fair was brilliant.
C: What rides did you go on?
D: (*loud*) That's why I need to borrow somebody's homework. I was there, went on all the rides.
A: (*interested*) Go on, tell me . . . which was the best ride?

And so on!

As a variation, ask your students to get into groups of three. Two students must try to ignore the third.
For example;

A: Great night last night.
B: What did you do?
C: (*ignores B*) I enjoyed it, too. Fantastic!
B: Did you go anywhere special?
A: (*to C*) We must go next week.
C: Costs though . . . but it's worth it.
B: Where did you go?
A: (*to C*) I liked the leader. He had some great ideas.
B: What *are* you talking about?
C: (*to A*) He's going to run through some of the techniques next week.
–And so on!

Forum Theatre

Forum Theatre is a form of drama in which the scene is enacted and watched by other members of the group. At any point in the drama, one of the actors can stop the action and ask for help or ideas to develop the action in a new direction.

Any member of the observing group (the audience) can step in and take over an existing role. A member of the observing group can add themselves in as an additional character. We have already looked at this with the 'Freeze and do' exercise.

Ask your students to try out one of the following situations:

a) A character is caught stealing secret documents from a military base. One of the military police might decide on extreme measures to interrogate the character. Another military policeman might wish to employ some moderate methods – and so a conflict might arise. As an argument ensues, the captured character might want to say something.

b) Two teachers and a parent have to decide what will happen to a disruptive student. The teachers hold different views as to how to deal with the student. The parent might think the student is not disruptive and has been dealt with in an unfair way.

You may wish to show an example from Scenario A, so that the students know what is expected from them.

> **Policeman 1:** This guy won't talk. He needs to be tortured.
>
> **Policeman 2:** (*firm*) Torture isn't civilised. It's against our code of practice.
>
> **Policeman 1:** Do you want this guy to go free?
>
> **Prisoner** (*quick*) I ain't no spy, gov. I was just curious . . . that's all.
>
> **Policeman 1:** (*laughs with scorn*) Am I expected to believe that? Bet you've got hundreds of secrets in that brain of yours. Bet you're ready to sell to the highest bidder. Well, I'll get those secrets out of you – one way or another!
>
> **Policeman 2:** You can't torture him . . . it's against the Geneva Convention.
>
> **Prisoner:** (*speaking fast*) No – you can't torture me. It ain't right. I demand to see my solicitor.
>
> **Policeman 1:** (*to the observing group, after a long pause*) Help me some-one. I can't think what to say next.
>
> **Sandy:** Tell the prisoner you don't care about protocol. He'll talk – you have ways and means.
>
> **Gareth:** Show him a torture implement. Say you'll use it if he won't speak.
>
> **Policeman 1:** Yeah! Good ideas! (*going back to the action and speaking to the prisoner*) Listen, I know you've got some of our secrets. I want to know who you work for. Tell me (*picks up a piece of rope*) or I'll find out the hard way.
>
> **Prisoner:** (desperate) You can't touch me!

Policeman 1: Can't I?

Daniel: (*entering acting area as an additional character*) Officer! What are you doing?

Policeman 2: (*pointing to policeman one*) He was going to torture this prisoner!

Carmen: (*enters the acting area and taps **Policeman 1** on the shoulder. She takes over the role. **Policeman 1** joins the observing group and **Carmen** becomes **Policeman 1**) So – how do *you* intend to find out the vital information we need?

Daniel (*as **Commanding Officer**, speaking to **Policeman 2***) Arrest this man!

Policeman 1: (*shocked*) Arrest me?

Your students may wish to continue this scenario and develop it in another way.

Forum Theatre is a powerful drama technique for improving a student's ability to think fast during role play. The collaboration between the actors and the observing group gives fresh interest, new storyline potential and a new impetus to the role-play activities. The group are able to help each other develop and expand their work.

For GCSE, students are encouraged to exchange ideas and learn from each other's work. It is essential that students watch and listen with care and observe all that is going on. In the above exercise, they are able to get involved and swap roles.

When the role play is complete, students should ask themselves the following questions.

- Did I or any member of the group make a useful suggestion when an actor asked for them?
- Did I or any member of the group take over an existing role or create a new one? Was the exchange or new character effective? Did the change move the drama along in any way?
- Did an interruption or change of actor make a **big** difference to the outcome of the play? Was the change an improvement and if so, how did it improve the outcome?

Still image

Ask your students what they believe a still image to be.

Tell them that still image is created when a group freeze mid-action, as if somebody has taken a photograph. Some drama teachers call still image a 'Freeze frame'. In my opinion, there is a distinction between the two.

A good still image will be carefully put together and should *tell* the audience a lot about what is happening. It should show the audience any tension between the characters or the situation.

A still image should have a sense of purpose. The 'picture' created should be important. It might be the moment when the action changes or it could be the most important part of the play or role play. Unlike when a director or a teacher shouts 'freeze' and the action halts and a student explains what is going on, a still image should be created by the actors involved in the action. They should decide upon their own pose, with feedback from the watching group. That is why, in my opinion, 'still image' differs from 'freeze framing'.

Ask your students to try one of the following still images. They will need to be in groups of four.

a) There has been a road accident. The onlookers are horrified. Some might be pointing, others weeping.
b) In a restaurant, a couple sit at a table. The waiter has just tripped and lurches towards the couple; the food tilted at a dangerous angle. Another customer looks on.
c) A sporting event. A goal has just been scored. Some spectators look happy, others look depressed. A pickpocket takes his opportunity!

Students can decide upon their main focus and adapt a, b and c as they wish. Having completed their still image, you can ask the actors what they hoped the watching group would focus on. Then ask the watching group what they thought the actors wanted them to focus on. If the two match, then the still image was a success.

Next, ask your students to try a sequence of still images that will tell a simple story. They can invent their own storyline but, if stuck, they could try one of the following;

Still 1: A and B meet and exchange a package. They are observed by C.
Still 2: C observes A, who has the package. A meets D.
Still 3: C observes D placing the package in a bin.
Still 4: C retrieves the package but is observed by A and D.
Still 5: C is lying sprawled on the floor and A has the package. D is standing over C's body and has a gun in his hand.

(Apologies to Geoffrey Chaucer)
Or:

Still 1: A and B have finished digging. They have discovered something (a chest of gold coins, perhaps). C and D observe and exchange glances.
Still 2: C and D have a gun pointing at A and B. B is holding the chest of gold coins.
Still 3: B hands the chest to C. D is laughing and A is dejected.
Still 4: C and D argue. The chest is on the ground, with the coins spilled on the floor. A and B observe.

Still 5: C and D lie on the ground, a gun in each hand. A and B are carrying the chest from the scene.

Allow your students to try these ideas in groups of four – or invent their own still image scenarios. Ask the observing groups if they understood the storylines from the still images. Get them to suggest how the still images could have been improved.

Now ask your students to think and develop a more complicated plot. They may need to be in groups of six or seven. This time, one of the group can act as a narrator and tell the story as the stills are put in place.

Check that your students have evaluated their work and the work of other groups. Each student needs to give some feedback to other members of his group and to other group members. Feedback could include the following;

- The still worked well because – (they need to give specific reasons).
- An improvement might be – (they need to give specific ideas).

Narrating: (I recommend this exercise for top GCSE candidates and for A/AS students.)

As we have just observed, narrating is allowing a spoken commentary alongside the action. It is like commenting at a sporting activity, such as at a tennis or football match. The commentary is happening alongside the action – they are both occurring at the same time.

The Greeks used a narrator to tell the story of a play, while actors mimed the action. This idea can be successful when working with your students because it allows them to develop other skills, such as facial expressions, body movements and use of acting space. To be a good narrator, students need to speak clearly and project their voice.

Ask your students to improvise one of the following;

1) A street, empty – except for an old man slumped in a doorway. He is occasionally drinking from a bottle. A young boy passes by – stops – looks hard at the old man and carries on. A young woman throws her wedding ring on the floor and sneers with disgust as she passes the old man. Finally, a couple walk past, the lady is carrying a baby. As they look at the drunk, they shake their heads sadly and peer down at the baby in the mother's arms.
2) A young man is playing a guitar. He is wearing a hoodie. A flat cap lies on the pavement. There are a few coins lying in it. A girl passes and she flicks a coin in the cap. They talk for a few brief moment, before she walks on. A policeman marches

briskly up to the young man. They exchange a few words. The policeman gestures that the young man must pack up and find somewhere else to sing. He stops playing, gathers his things and prepares to move on. He looks dejected.

Both 1 and 2 are open to interpretation. Your students will now need to improvise or script the narration. The action must be mimed. In groups of four or five, the students will need to choose a narrator.

You might wish to show them the example below.

From the first scenario:

(Student Narrating)

Observe the old drunkard. He's alone in the rough part of town on a cold winter's night. The wind blows late leaves and the day's dirt and sweet wrappings scud around him like lost dreams. Dreams half thought through and never quite grasped.

Who is that boy, fleetingly watching as the old drunkard swigs from his disgusting bottle? Why, it is himself – the happy boy, rosy-cheeked and full of young confidence. A boy who could have made something of his life. A boy full of potential – growing to a man who lost his way.

Now here comes a fine young woman . . . a wife! A treasure who needed warmth and kindness and devotion. Someone to share life's adventures, joys and trials. But demon drink ruined it all and she was forced to leave.

Look at the proud couple with their firstborn. They have a healthy young baby – a boy. They are saddened by their glimpse of the future.

What happened, old man? Why didn't you take the world by storm? Why didn't you take the life planned out for you? Ah, drink!

Another form of narrating, is for an actor to step out of the play and tell the audience what is going on, or to fill the gaps in the story. Your students might like to try this out for themselves. Using the ideas already given (or making up a story of their own) they can script the action, and a student can narrate any gaps.

Here is an example from the second scenario.

The action is taking place and the policeman has arrived. Tom (the *young man) steps out of the action and speaks directly to the audience.*

Like my singing do you? Haven't made much money have I? Helena, the girl, wanted to know how much I'd made. Not a lot – as you can see from the few coins in that old flat cap. She had the cheek to tell me I can't play or sing in tune. Still, she flicked 10 pence into the cap. Well, she was a real confidence booster . . . not! Now the copper is standing over me like a rock of doom.

(The mime continues and as Tom prepares to move on, he steps out of the mime again.)

Told me to pack up and move on. Apparently a VIP is on her way over. They want me out of the way. They don't want the unloved to dirty their proud streets. I'll find a patch near the river – you sometimes get rich pickings down there.

It wasn't always like this, you know. There was a time when I had a good job. That was before I met Ken and Melissa . . .

Your students might wish to continue this piece of drama.

Point out to your students that Shakespeare often used narration to explain what was happening in his plays. Ask them to look at 'Romeo and Juliet'. The prologue is the opening of the play. Here, a number of actors called a chorus summarize the play for the audience. Ask your class to divide into groups of four and work together to produce the prologue. Then ask them to work out what is happening, get into groups of eight and mime the action while the chorus speak the words in unison.

The Prologue.
Enter Chorus.
Two households, both alike in dignity,
In fair Verona, where we lay our scene,
From ancient grudge break to new mutiny,
Where civil blood makes civil hands unclean.
From forth the fatal loins of these two foes
A pair of star-cross'd lovers take their life;
Whose misadventur'd piteous overthrows
Doth with their death bury their parents' strife.
The fearful passage of their death-mark'd love,
And the continuance of their parents' rage,
Which, but their children's end, nought could remove,
Is now the two hours' traffic of our stage;
The which if you with patient ears attend,
What here shall miss, our toil shall strive to mend.

Sometimes Shakespeare had a narrator telling part of the tale, such as the porter in 'Macbeth'.

The narrator is speaking to himself but the words are intended for an audience.

Porter: Here's a knocking indeed! If a man were porter of hell-gate, he
should have turned old turning the key. (*Knock*) Knock, knock, knock!
Who's there, i'th' name of Beelzebub? Here's a farmer that hang'd
himself on th' expectation of plenty. Come in time; have napkins enow

about you; here you'll sweat for't. (*Knock*) Knock, knock! Who's there, i' th' other devil's name? Faith, here's an equivocator, that could swear in both scales against either scale; who committed treason enough for God's sake, yet could not equivocate to heaven. O, come in, equivocator. (*Knock*) Knock, knock, knock! Who's there? Faith, here's an English tailor come hither for stealing out of a French hose. Come in, tailor, here you may roast your goose. (*Knock*) Knock, knock; never at quiet! What are you? But this place is too cold for hell. I'll devil-porter it no further. I had thought to have let in some of all professions that go the primrose way to th' everlasting bonfire. (*Knock*) Anon, anon! (*Opens the gate*)I pray you remember the porter.

Tell your students that Macbeth has just killed King Duncan. The porter's speech brings some light relief to the audience but the knocking comes from the hand of Macduff, who kills Macbeth towards the end of the play.

Here, the porter is imagining himself to be the porter at the gates of hell. This is irony, as the killing of a king was seen to be against God's established order.

Remind your students that an equivocator is a double-dealer. The English tailor stole French cloth to make fashionable clothes. These people, according to the porter, have reached the gates of hell.

Now ask your students to get into groups of four or five and mime the porter scene while one of the group speaks the words.

Hot seating

I use hot seating to allow students to question characters in role. I usually ask a student to sit in a chair, which is the 'hot seat'. The group can sit in a semi-circle and ask questions. In a classroom situation, the group can sit at desks and the student can sit in the teacher's chair. When questions are asked, the student needs to remain in character.

Hot seating can be used for improvisation. This enables the group to understand more about a particular character. They can also understand the character's motives for behaving or acting in a certain way. Hot seating can also be used to discover how much a student really knows about a particular character or situation in a play they have studied in drama.

Hot seating is useful because it forces the student in the hot seat to think quickly. It also makes the questioners think of an appropriate question that will need a considered response. I have been surprised as to how often students will look at a character or a situation in an original and imaginative way. They might explore ideas that I had not thought about! I trust you will find the same!

Students in the hot seat need to know about the person they are 'being'. If you are studying a play and the answers are inaccurate, you might need to step in! With some groups, it might be appropriate for you to take the hot seat and allow students the opportunity to formulate and ask questions. This method enables you to get them to discover more about a character – but in a creative way!

There are different forms of hot seating that you might like to try with your students.

- The action of a character can be questioned by other characters from the play or improvisation. In this form of hot seating, everyone keeps in role but not from a scene in the play or improvisation. Students might like to add characters who are not in the play – for example an imaginary sibling or a former friend of the character in the hot seat. As an example, Macbeth is in the hot seat, having made sure Macduff's wife and children have been murdered.

Macduff: Why did you murder my wife and children?

Macbeth: I saw you as a threat to my throne. I guessed you intended to plot against me. You'd gone to the English court for help. I had to deal with you in some way – show you I meant business.

Macduff's Sister: What made you pay soldiers to murder innocent women and children?

Macbeth: I had allowed evil to enter me. Remember, I'd already had my best friend murdered. (*pause*) I thought I was invincible.

Malcolm: You received false information from the witches, didn't you?

Macbeth: Yes.

Malcolm: Can you describe exactly what happened when you met the witches?

(*Macbeth describes the event.*)

Lady Macbeth: Talk about our relationship. How did it deteriorate? Why didn't you tell me exactly what was going on? Why didn't you tell me you wanted to murder Banquo and his son? Why did you keep me in the dark?

Another form of hot seating is to allow several students to be in the hot seat at once. With this method, you can allow the actors to debate with each other in front of their questioners.

Imagine a group has just performed an improvisation involving a car accident.

Questioner: (*to the driver*) How much alcohol had you drunk before you took to the wheel?

Driver: (*hesitates*) I can't remember.

Questioner 2: But . . . you were well over the limit?

Driver: (*hesitates again*) Y . . . yes.

Mother: (*angry*) Don't you think your behaviour was totally irresponsible?

Driver: I didn't think so at the time.

Mother: Because you were out to impress your mates! What was the result of that, eh? The result is, my son lies injured in a hospital bed!

Questioner 3: (*to mother*) But **you** let him play on a busy road – all by himself.

Driver: So the accident wasn't entirely my fault.

Mother: (*to the group*) What am I supposed to do? I've got three toddlers and a baby to look after. (*to driver*) **You** only have yourself to please.

Scruff: (*driver's friend, to mother*) But you have to admit your responsibility.

Questioner 4: (*to driver*) Can you go over the events that led up to your drinking spree. Hadn't your girlfriend just dumped you?

Notice the interaction between the questioners and the characters in the hot seats. Notice also, the characters' interaction with each other. The questions are probing and they indicate that all the participants know the improvisation.

A final form of hot seating is to arrange the events as a courtroom scene. For example, Macbeth might be on trial for killing King Duncan. Or you could devise the hot seating as a police interrogation. For example, imagine the character, Othello is interrogated for murdering his wife, Desdemona.

Successful hot seating depends upon the type of questions asked. Make sure you allow your students plenty of preparation time for the type of questions they can ask. It is good to start with 'Why did you . . . ?' or 'What made you . . . ?' These questions relax the student in the hot seat and give that student something to talk about. However, questioners can then probe deeper. Students can then ask moral questions such as, 'How could you . . . ?'

If you want to know how much a student knows about a particular play, you could encourage the questioners to ask probing questions such as 'Tell me about . . . ?' or 'Go through the events that led up to . . . ?' Or, 'What do you think is really going on in this situation . . . ?'

Other probing questions might be; 'Why didn't you . . . ?' Or 'Did you expect (*a particular character*) to act in that way.' Or 'Why did you (*say and/or act*) when . . . ?'

The probing questions allow the student in the hot seat to think deeper. It also has the advantage that you get to know how much a particular student or a group has understood about a character and/or a situation or a play. When performing improvisations, you get to know how much a group has really organized and thought through scenarios.

It is good practice to allow your students to evaluate the use of hot seating. You might like to ask them the following questions;

- Did this exercise allow you to understand the character in a deep and more meaningful way? If so, give some examples.
- Did the exercise make you change your mind about a character in the play or the play as a whole?

Cross-cutting

The idea of cross-cutting is to reorder a sequence of events in a piece of drama. The action can go forwards into the future or cut backwards to an earlier time in the play. Your students might start with a middle scene and then flash forward to a later scene or flash back to an earlier scene . . . and continue with the final scene. This technique takes students away from linear action and is a technique often used in films. Ask your students to think of a film they have recently seen that uses flashbacks or flash forwards. A comparatively old example of films that use this technique are the three *Back To The Future* films, especially *Back To The Future 2*. A modern example is *Inception*, and the *Lost* series from television, which uses both flashbacks and flash forwards in an imaginative and inventive way.

Below is a drama sequence that was the result of a piece of improvisation.

Scene 1: Greg and Alex are preparing to climb a high mountain. An experienced climber at the local cafe warns them not to climb as the weather will turn bad and the mountain top is dangerous when the mist descends.

Scene 2: Greg and Alex meet with Basaam and Aaheli, who warn them that the mist is coming down. Basaam and Aaheli beg Greg and Alex to come down with them. Greg and Alex are more determined than ever to climb to the mountain top.

Scene 3: Greg and Alex are lost in thick fog. Alex almost falls to her death but Greg rescues her. They are both scared and cold and frightened. They lament the fact that they'd not heeded anyone's advice.

Scene 4: Mountain rescuers find Greg and Alex, who are dangerously close to a precipice. They are taken down the mountain and reunited with Basaam and Aaheli, who raised the alarm.

For a cross-cut, your students might start with Scene Three, go back to Scene One and two and end with Scene Four.

The use of cross-cutting is to show a different perspective on the narrative. Cross cutting can keep the audience engaged and, as the play can open at a point of high drama (Greg and Alex lost in fog), the audience is immediately engaged.

Ask your students to use the following scenario to create their own cross cutting.

> Scene One: An adventure group go pot holing. They are warned that the water levels in the caves are rising due to heavy rain.
> Scene Two: Four friends are lost down the pot hole and are trapped in a narrow tunnel when there is a landfall.
> Scene Three: The friends attempt to crawl back to the entrance hole but fear they will drown as the water levels are now dangerous.
> Scene Four: Experienced pot holers are called and rescue the friends just in time!

Ask your students to improvise the scene, deciding when to start (which scene) and when to finish!

Theatre is not the same as film and instant flashbacks or flash forwards are not possible. There are some interesting techniques your students might like to try. There are;

Parallel cross-cutting – through mime and acting

While performing a scene from the middle of a narrative, but at the start of the play, some of the actors could mime scene one at the same time. The characters might appear in both scenes, but could be played by different actors.

Greg and Alex could be lost in thick fog and talking about the old man's advice. They might wish they'd listened to him. Now they are cold and think they might die on the mountain top.

At the same time, perhaps behind them or to the right of the stage, Greg and Alex mime listening to the old man, who could be pointing to the mountain and shaking his head.

Use still image *and* narrative

While a scene is being performed, a character could 'step out' of the action (which then freezes) and explain what has happened earlier – for example there has just been a car accident. A boy is injured and his mum is crying. Two boys step from the car, they are unsure of their step. They look as if they have come from a party. The action freezes and the mother explains to the audience that the boys had drunk too much alcohol at a party. The driver's girlfriend had just finished their relationship and he was drowning his sorrows.

Unfortunately, the consequence of their drinking was the injuring of her young son.

Ask your students to improvise and try out the above technique. They can work in small groups.

Cross-cutting ideas

Ask your students to get into small groups of about three or four. When in groups, ask them to create and improvise a piece in sequence. Get them to write down their ideas as four or five continuous scenes. As they script the piece, they might consider how to improve it.

Once they have written it down, ask them to act it out in normal time. When a group is happy with their performance (and you are, too), they can experiment and reorder the scenes so that the play can be seen in a different way, perhaps with a new emphasis. Encourage them to use a combination of mime and action, or still images and narration. If stuck, students can use one of the following three scenarios.

1) Jasmine, Brian, Damien and Cheryl are survivors of a shipwreck. They manage to spot an island. They land on the island and work out ways to survive. They need to find or build shelter and discover food and fresh water. After a short while, they realize they are being watched. A group of men, dressed in white coats, arrest them. In a dungeon on the island, the four children work out a way to escape.

2) Tasha is abducted by aliens. Her mum and sister watch in horror as she is bundled inside a spacecraft. Inside the spacecraft, Tasha meets Carl, who has also been abducted. They notice the aliens observing them. The aliens are copying their speech. At first, they get some words wrong but they quickly improve and soon they have mastered the English language. They inform Tasha and Carl that they intend to invade Earth. Tasha and Carl need to escape, to warn others about the intended invasion.

3) Simon and Cherry find a small bottle lying on the roadside. They shake the bottle and a voice answers – telling them not to shake the bottle but to rub it! Soon a Genie appears and grants them both three wishes – which they must decide on together. After a debate, Simon and Cherry decide on riches, fame and a large house with a swimming pool. The Genie laughs. The two-some find themselves on stage holding a microphone. They are a laughing stock. They know they've just messed up a song on a talent show. However, they are

signed on as a comedy act. Soon they have so much money and they don't know what to do with it. They are unhappy – they want their old lives back. They search in vain for the Genie.

Once the cross cutting has taken place, ask your students to evaluate how it worked. What might they do differently next time? How might they make the cross cutting more complex but still understandable.

CHAPTER 3

Stimulating drama

Music

Music is excellent for creating atmosphere. Students can be encouraged to open and close a piece of improvisation with music. Use of music in this context allows a piece of improvisation to 'hang together'. The lyric, tempo and style of music can be carefully chosen to underline the **theme** of the improvisation. I have always found the students are much better at choosing music for an improvisation than I am!

Music can be used as background – but it isn't useful if it drowns out the spoken word. There is nothing worse for an audience than watching a play and the music is so obtrusive that those performing the play cannot be heard.

Ask your students to write an improvised scene then choose and use an appropriate piece of music to go with their work. When they have worked in a group and achieved their goal, ask them to find a piece of music that is appropriate as a background to their work. Most students enjoy choosing music as a piece of homework.

Sound cues

It is possible to buy sound cues that are professionally made. The biggest factor for a full production or a short script is that the student in charge of the sound cue comes in at the right time! That is, unless you are using mistimed sound cues as part of a parody/comedy. It really is a good idea to have a technical rehearsal to ensure that the cues work correctly. Some writers show the cues on a script but it is also a good idea to write a cue sheet.

Here is a short script with a writer's suggestions for music and cues. Ask your students to work through the script and find appropriate music and sound effects for the sound cues.

'Secrets' by Georgina Wiggins

(The scene opens with soft music – fading as the actors begin to talk.)

Harry: Well, Cath – here's the old haunted house.

Cathy: I came here a long time ago. This was my grandma's house.

Harry: *(scrunches up the gravel)* The place is empty and ruined now. *(footsteps on gravel)*

Cathy *(laughs)* See those high turrets? Grandma would never let me climb the stairs to any of those four turrets.

Harry: *(interested)* Why?

Cathy: *(an owl hoots – she hesitates)* She claims it was haunted. *(as she speaks, an owl screeches)* What was that?

Harry: Only an owl. You nervous?

Cathy: *(laughs quickly)* Nervous . . . yes, I suppose I am.

(They reach the front door. Harry bangs loudly on the thick wooden door.)

Cathy: Reminds me of a poem we studied at school. Think it was called 'The Listeners.' It's about somebody returning to a house they once lived in, only years later. Nobody lived in that old house anymore. But the lost, dead years – or ghosts – were listening. Later, when the traveller banged on the door . . .

Harry: *(interrupting)* You and your imagin . . .

(The door creaks open) Hello?

Butler: You called, Sir?

(Behind the butler, there is the sound of somebody frantically moving something heavy in the hallway – followed by the sound of brushing.)

Encourage your students to write a cue sheet. Cues need to be listed in order. Next to each cue should be the dialogue or action. This indicates when the sound should be produced. Here is a start, using the above script.

Cue Number	Cue	Details	Time Allocated
Cue 1	Soft music.	Steve's guitar solo.	Fade after thirty seconds.
Cue 2	This was my grandma's house.	Sound of crunching gravel.	Fade after fifteen seconds.
Cue 3	Let's explore	walking on gravel.	Fifteen seconds.

Students are good at creating their own sound effects. For example, Cue 1 was Steve playing his guitar. Rain, for example, can be created by rubbing hands together and crunching gravel is made by rustling sweet papers. The students usually create their own imaginative sound effects – much better than my suggestions!

Symbols

Props can represent symbols. For example, the empty cross is a Christian symbol representing the resurrection of Jesus. The cross was used in the film 'Fireproof' as a background image when a father talked to his son about love and commitment.

The symbol of a crow can be used to indicate death or future destruction.

Symbols should not be too obscure but easily recognized by the audience to give them a non-verbal clue as to what is happening in a particular scene. For example, if a scene opened with a woman kneeling by a gravestone in a church yard with a picture of a man in uniform in her hand, the audience might reasonably conclude that her husband or lover had died.

A clever group of students might use symbols for effect. For instance, a bell slowly ringing might indicate death. If a bird screeches past a couple while they are having their wedding photographs taken, the bird symbol might indicate future unhappiness.

Objects can be used as symbols. A bare rock, centre stage, might indicate hardship. In the film (and book) *Lord of the Flies* the conch is a symbol of order and authority. It becomes more than just a shell. In *Waiting For Godot* Estragon's struggle with his boots indicates a sense of hopelessness.

Allow your students to annotate the script below, putting in appropriate sound cues and noting the symbols used, where appropriate.

Before the match
(Three friends are in Ossie's lounge.)

Ossie: I got a feeling we're going to win today.

Lena: (*shakes her head*) I don't think so (*hesitates*). Not so sure I'm going to join you guys today. I promised I'd meet some of the girls from work. We're going to lose this one.

Cuth: (*fiddles with a coin in his hand*) We're going to win, Lena. You a supporter or what?

Ossie: (*flicks coin, it lies heads upwards in his palm*) She's thinking we're going to miss those old crocks we sold to City.

Lena: Experience, that's what counts. We sold two experienced defenders. (*She glances at an old faded photograph of the F.A. Cup winning team.*)

Ossie: An old team never won anything! (*He glances at a photograph of the youth team, holding the Youth Cup in their hands.*) You wait and see, our youth policy will work.

Lena: (*standing up*) But boys – we haven't won a match this season!

Cuth: (*to Ossie*) We'd better get going. We'll be late.
(*Cuth opens the front door. The rain is pouring down.*)
Ossie: (*to Lena*) We're taking on the league leaders, it'll be an exciting match.
Cuth: (*glancing at the coin in his hand*) The turning point of the season.
Lena: I don't think so boys. I'm not watching another hammering; I'm
     going to join the girls in the cafe. Join us when you're 6–0 down!

If your students are stuck, ask them what is the significance of the coin or
the two photographs. What might these represent? What about the rain
(*technically pathetic fallacy*), does this suggest the team will win or lose?

Television and film

I have already mentioned some aspects of drama relating to television and film. Students are keenly aware of the two. I have generally
discovered that students enjoy writing television and film scripts.

When writing television scripts, your students need to know that
television is about sight and sound. Most students, if they think
about it, already know this. However, they find it very tempting to
write long passages of script as in a stage play. They do need to bear
in mind that the vision and not the script comes first. They need
to think visually. They need to remember that the viewer is looking at a television and not a stage! On stage, this is not important.
The audience will focus on listening to what the characters are saying. On stage, for obvious reasons, there isn't too much action. Most
stage plays are probably over 90% talk. The majority of television
programmes (fiction) are under 50% talk – because there is so much
else to see. Often, a television scriptwriter will write in incidents
that happen in silence – when a character is alone.

Silent patches are very common in television. They can have
a powerful impact. For example, an old lady might pick up a
photograph of a long dead relative, look at the photograph, smile
sadly and place the photograph on the shelf. You might then see her
lip quiver, as though she's about to cry. She might shake her head,
grab a duster and dust around the mantelpiece. Nothing is spoken,
but much is 'said'.

Generally speaking, television series deals with the here and now –
although there are obvious exceptions. It deals with 'real' people in
'real' situations. There isn't yet a soap opera set in the past or in the
future. They are all set in the present. Therefore, the backgrounds
are all ones that most students can identify with. Ask your students
to watch a soap opera (or show one) and get them to check the storylines. There are often a number of storylines happening at once. Ask
your students how real the storylines feel. Do they think the storylines are realistic? Could the events in the soap opera happen to
them? If so, the scriptwriter has succeeded.

A golden rule of scriptwriting for television is that the writing is restricted to no more than four characters per scene. Ask your students to watch an episode of a soap opera and get them to check how many characters are used per scene at any one time! This excludes background characters, in a shop or pub or in the street. Of course, there are always exceptions! The golden rule is broken if you have one person talking to a crowd, or a mob descending on a police station, with many characters speaking at once. The golden rule is broken sparingly and when broken, television scenes quickly return to the norm – which is two or three important characters (four at the most) per scene. Often, these characters are viewed in close-up.

Television allows close-ups, so facial expressions are used for effect – remember the old lady with her trembling lip!

Your students need to know when writing for television, that speeches are short and as few as possible. There are, as always, exceptions – but these are exceptions rather than the norm.

Another obvious point is that television rarely uses a narrator in fiction. Who people are and what relationship they are to each other needs to be made clear very quickly. Where each scene takes place needs to be obvious, too.

Your students need to know the following, when writing dialogue for television –

- The characters' ages, education and background need to be obvious very quickly.
- How are the characters meant to speak? Do they speak differently when angry or upset?
- Avoid unnecessary dialogue . . . when used it **must** move the plot forward.
- Characters do not need to **explain** their feelings. It is much better that their feelings are explained through their actions.
- Avoid any long speeches. The speeches can be broken up by allowing other characters to interrupt or by actions that are relevant to the scene.
- Avoid characters talking to themselves.

Ask your students to read through the three short television scenes. Two are not suitable for television but one might be suitable. Can your students spot which two are wrong and why? There might be more than one reason.

Your students should reflect on;

- The characters' body language. Are they meant to be aggressive, upset, flippant or what?
- How should the characters deliver their lines? What tone of voice does each character need? What intonation? Which words do characters need to emphasize?

If possible, your students could read and act out Scenarios A, B and C. That might give them a better understanding of what might or might not work.

Script A. *Ext: Open field.* Night sky. Terry looks up into the night sky. He sees something that resembles a flying saucer.

Terry (*talking to himself*) Well, I'll be dog gone . . . wait till the boys hear this!

(*Cut to internal. Pub, 'The Hungry Bear'*)

Landlord: (*to Anika*) What's kept Terry? (*glances at watch*). He's usually here by now.

Anika: (*glances down at an empty glass*) Who cares. Do you want to know something? My pet white rabbit named Drift – get it . . . white, snow drift . . . has had babies. Eight in all! Four white – but one of those might be grey – and four black. When I say black, one might be a sort of charcoal colour. Pregnant? I didn't even know next doors buck had escaped. They were very shifty when I asked. Must have been when I was in the South of France – anyway, as I was saying . . .

Landlord: (*head in hands*) Interesting.

(*The pub door swings open. Terry stands there, looking like a nightmare from somebody's dream.*)

Terry: (*hot and bothered*) Aliens . . . I've seen them. They're landing here in the field up the road.

Landlord: (*shakes his head*) Usual, Terry?

Terry: (*upset*) You don't believe me, do you?

Anika: (*looking down at her nails*) Want a rabbit, Terry?

(*At that moment, three aliens burst into the pub.*)

Alien 1: Don't move!

Alien 2: Resistance is futile.

Alien 3: Move and you die.

Script B: *Int: Classroom. The classroom is empty except for Rosalia, Karen and Lilly. Rosalia and Karen are standing over Lilly in an intimidating manner. Lilly is sitting meekly at her desk, looking up at them.*

Rosalia: So you want to fit in, eh?

Karen: (*to Rosalia*) Course she wants to fit in, natural ain't it?

Rosalia: (*to Lilly*) So you'll do something for us, eh?

Lilly: (*not quite understanding*) Yes, I want to be your friend.

Rosalia: So you'll steal Miss Hay's money?

(*silence*)

Karen: Well?

Cut to int: Rosalia's house. The Holtby's kitchen. It is in a state of disarray. Rosalia is peering into the fridge. Her mum is banging her fist on the microwave. Frank is pouring himself a coffee.

Frank: (*to Rosalia's back*) So, you going to get that Chinese girl to nick the money or what?

Rosalia: (*turns from the fridge to look at Frank*) Don't know. Not for sure.

(*Rosalia bangs the fridge door shut with her heel.*)

Frank: You owe me, sis.

Rosalia: (*angry burst of temper*) Yeah and don't you keep reminding me!

Mrs Holtby: (*glaring at the defunct microwave*) Will you two shut it! Can't hear myself think! (*she bangs the microwave one last time*) And this thing don't work no more. You two been messing with it?

Frank: No, mum.

(*Rosalia opens the fridge again and takes out a yoghurt. Frank looks at her and laughs.*)

Is that all you're eating, sis?

Rosalia: (*rubs her hands gently over her body*) Got to keep my figure.

Frank: Who for? From what I've heard, Jason don't love you no more.

(*Rosalia throws the unopened yoghurt pot, full force, at Frank. He ducks and the yoghurt pot bursts open as it hits the wall. Rosalia storms out of the room and slams the door behind her.*)

Mrs Holtby: (*to Frank*) Now look what you've done!

Frank: She still owes me, Mum, she still owes me!

Script C: *Ext: Ploughed field. Two boys are running across a field. They run to the edge of the field. They stop, panting, doubled over, gasping for breath. They are dressed as boys from the 1970s.*

Steve: Phew – that was close.

Baz: Didn't know old Farmer Carter kept a bull in his field.

Steve: I was **scared**. For the first time in ages . . . I mean **really** scared.

Baz: (*thinking*) Makes you wonder how they do it in Spain, in places like Pamplona. You know – the bull fighters. How do they **face** those big bulls?

Narrator: Baz knew the matadors do face the bulls in Pamplona. He'd been there, seen the bulls run through the streets, seen a goring incident. The memory made him shudder. However, he had other worries now he'd escaped the farmer's bull.

Baz: What are we going to do about old Wilkie?

Steve: (*laughs*) Set a bull on him?

Baz: You never know, he might not be in tomorrow.

(*Fade to school classroom.*)

Mr Wilkinson: (*glancing through a pile of books*) Steven Morecroft?

Steve: Yes, sir.

Mr Wilkinson: Where's your homework, Moron?

Steve: (*stuttering*) Er – I did do it sir. Got chased by a bull and . . .

Mr Wilkinson: Morecroft, Moron (*the class laugh*) I don't want to know all your problems . . . I just want your homework, boy!

(*Fade to the interior of Steve's house. He is now middle aged and a boy is sitting next to him. The boy is dressed as a modern teenager.*)

Matt: So then what happened, dad?

Steve: I was caned (*ruffles the boy's hair*) that's what it was like in my day, Matt.

Matt: (*chewing gum*) Tell me another story, dad.

Your students should note that Script A is inappropriate because of the introduction of aliens and the long irrelevant speech about rabbits. This script is redeemable. Perhaps, if Terry thought he'd seen a spaceship and no aliens appeared – and the speech about rabbits was shorter and broken up (to show something about Anika's character) it might work. The script could focus on Terry's imagination and could be quite a comic situation. Perhaps the aliens were fundraisers, dressed up. The thing that looked like a spaceship could be a coincidence.

Script B would work, as it was set in the present and dealt with a subject that most people would find easily identifiable. The family in the second scene were obviously a dysfunctional family.

Script C would need a lot of work to become a possible television script. Your students should note that it was set in the 1970s, used a narrator and changed times. Where would the script go? Perhaps it could be set in the present, with a focus on the homework problem?

Now ask your students to write two short scenes for television, or revise and re-write Scripts A or C. When complete, the scenes could be acted out with other groups becoming the audience and later feeding back with constructive criticism.

Film

When writing scripts for film, it is worth noting that one minute of screen time would take up one typed script page. There are screenplay terms that your students might like to note. These are;

V.O. which stands for **voiceover**. Voiceover is narration that does not come from the scene itself. It can be a narrator or the inner thoughts of a character on screen. Alternatively, it can be a voice coming over a radio or a loud speaker which the filmmaker can add in later.

O.S. This means **off screen**. Any dialogue or sound that is heard in the scene but is not actually seen. For example, a boss might be shouting at an employee but the employee might be locked inside a broom cupboard. The boss might then hammer on the cupboard door but all we see is the employee covered in brooms, cringing.

P.O.V. This is short for **Point of View**. This technique shows a scene from the point of view of a particular character. For example, a young woman might witness a murder but we see it from a chink in the door that the young woman is looking through, as if we have her eyes.

Series of shots: This is used to show us varied shots and locations which can be used to **establish a scene or a sense of place**. For example, if an action takes place in the remote highlands of Scotland, you might see a shot of a piper dressed in a kilt. The next shot might be of a mountain range, suggesting the highlands of Scotland. The third shot could be that of a ruined castle with the mountains in the background. Finally, a shot of the banqueting hall with people eating a meal. By the time the characters have been shown, you know the setting and place – without a word spoken!

Re: is short for '**reference to**'. This is useful when several characters are speaking to each other or when referring to props or objects. For example;

> Jamie Knight
>
> (re: the body on the floor)
>
> This is bad. Very bad. What happens now?

The Royal 'We'. Try to avoid the Royal We as much as possible. As in 'We see' or 'We hear'.

So, encourage your students to write, 'Thunder rolled ominously and lightning struck a tree in the far distance' rather than 'We hear thunder and we see lightening strike a tree in the far distance.'

A further look at voiceover

Voiceovers go with images for television programmes (very often, for adverts). The way a voiceover is written can affect the meaning of an image.

Ask your students to look at three voiceovers about a film that is advertised at the local cinema. The film is a cartoon. Which voiceover do they feel is the most effective and why?

Still of a beetle and a ladybird. The beetle appears to be squashing the ladybird. In the distance is a grasshopper wearing a cowboy hat. The grasshopper holds a gun.

Voiceover One: Jessie Hardcastle is a beetle bully. Watch as he tries to crush the life and soul out of Dotty Ladybird and everyone else in Dumpsville. However, Harry Hero the grasshopper is about to change everything!

Voiceover Two: A big beetle bullies a small ladybird as our hero grasshopper waits in the distance.

Voiceover Three: Big beetle Jessie gets what he wants in Dumpsville. Anyone in his way cops it . . . until Sheriff Harry Hero arrives.

Your students should work out that Voiceover One works best as it gives the audience more information.

Show your students a television advert and then still a frame. Ask your students to write their own voiceover for that still. Then show them two more frames for the same advert and ask them to write two more stills. They can then record their own voiceovers. Now ask them to write their own advert and draw three stills. They can then write their own voiceovers and record the voiceovers.

How to set out a film script

'Jack's Jobs'

Int: The Happy Hare – Evening.

As Jack heads for the table, he slips and the food slides from the plate and onto the tray.

Jack

I'm not cut out for this job. I'm not meant to be a waiter.

Woman

You are so clumsy, young man.

Jack Scowls.

Jack

And you are so ugly. I won't be clumsy for ever but you . . .

Woman screams. Jack drops the tray on the floor, food-side down. Jack heads for the exit door. Once through the door, he quickly takes off his jacket and flings it onto the ground, stamping it into the ground with his feet.

O.S. Woman calls for the manager.

Your students should note that internal (Int) and external (ext) are the same as in a script for television. However, when writing a film script, the character's name is set in the middle of the page. The dialogue is underneath the name. Any stage directions (Jack Scowls . . .) is written at the left hand of the page.

Tell your students never to say 'The Camera . . . ' but make it obvious what the camera has to do (Jack heads for the exit door . . .)

Now ask your students to write a scene or two for a screenplay and then, if possible, act out and film the scenes. They must set out the script as in the example above.

If stuck, here are three possible plots for a script.

Plot One: Two girls find a boy with blood on his face. He admits he has been joy riding with his friends, he's a T.W.O.C. The car crashed and he got out. The police are tracking him. What do the girls do?

Plot Two: A couple find a boy who does not appear to understand them. They are outside a busy motorway cafe. They look round for any adults whom the boy might belong to. It is night, the boy shivers. He might be abandoned. What do they do?

Plot Three: Simon finds a girl trapped down a pothole. The girl explains
   that she was out walking when the rain poured down. The ground
   opened up, she fell down and now her legs are pinned. Does he go for
   help or carry on talking to her, hoping that somebody else turns up?
   She's in obvious pain and discomfort.

Writing for radio

Radio scripts have been written, performed and perfected for over
eighty years. They are written in a particular tried and tested way.
Ask your students to look at the sample script but read the following
first of all;

- A page needs to be uncrowded. The double-spacing between
  lines and the wide margin means that everything is clear.
- The character's name is always to the left of the page. The
  speakers' names are always in capital letters.
- Everything that is not spoken is underlined. This makes it much
  easier for the actors to see their speeches.
- All that is heard, apart from the speeches, is called the
  effects. The effects are shown by the letter FX. This is also
  shown on the left-hand column.
- Your students know this fact – but it is worth a mention – the
  only thing coming from a radio play is sound. Description is
  out, unless you want a character to describe something.
- In radio, because you cannot see the characters, their names
  must be made clear early on. For example;

DAD. What are you doing, Jenny?
JENNY. Sorry dad, won't keep you for long.

Places also need to be made clear. Perhaps the sound of waves or the
   cry of seagulls to show that the action takes place at a seaside. Or
   the buzz of traffic and clank of plates to suggest a motorway cafe.
   Birds singing and the moo of a cow could suggest a country setting.
   Another way to suggest place and setting is for a character to make
   it obvious through speech.
For example:

DANIELLE. I hate the country. The grasses make my hay fever bad.
GEMMA. So, why are we here? Why did you bring us to Little
   Cranford?
Or;
DAVE. Where will we find the little squirt?
MAUREEN. Behind the bike shed. He's always there.
DAVE. Come on then – let's get him before he disappears. (*fading*)
The clank of bikes unlocked and taken from their stands.

Narration can be used effectively in radio – remember not to use narration when writing television scripts.

NARRATOR. They arrived in Cherbourg on a cold, windy morning. Dawn had come but they were too early for the cafe. Besides, Tina still felt sea-sick and the idea of food made her stomach churn. They didn't spot Louis, although he was watching them. All of a sudden his promises seemed as cold and dismal as this early morning. Tina turned and glanced at Michelle. Michelle would know what to do. (*fade*)

FX *French music playing. A group of Frenchmen speaking in the background.* The sound of boat masts clanking in the wind.

LOUIS. Ah, Tina, you will return, won't you? I need you!

- When writing radio plays, you can use many people. However, you need to keep the main characters to the minimum. You are free to use a number of minor characters. This is because an actor can read three or four parts of a radio play. Remember, you do not see the actors – you just hear them.

For example;

FX *The sound of busy traffic.*
LOUIS. So, this is London, eh? C'est La Vie.
TINA. Yes, this is the place where it all happens. You've never been to London before?
LOUIS. Non. Pour certainment, non. Jamais. (*fading*)
GEORGINA. Hear that? He claims this is his first visit. The liar.
Ist POLICEMAN. Thanks, Georgina. That's all we need to know.
2nd POLICEMAN. The rogue. We'll arrest him now. We have enough evidence.
3rd POLICEMAN. Let's do it.
GEORGINA. No, wait – I don't want Tina harmed.

Point out to your students that;

- Scenes start and end with fading. Fading simply means the volume is turned up or down. This means scenes can fade in (volume up) or out (volume down). When listeners hear voices fading up or down they know a scene is starting or a scene is over. A new scene begins with a fade up and a scene ends with a fade down.
- Some scenes have pointers to show what will happen in the following scene. The scene should not fade down when a pointer is happening, so that a listener fails to hear a pointer. Below is an example of how it can be done;

DAD. Fine, I'll go and sort it out.
ERIC. You don't mean . . .

> DAD. I mean I'm going to see your head teacher. I'm going to walk
>   right into her office and ask for an explanation.
> ERIC. But dad . . . (*fade*)

Ask your students to identify the pointer (I'm going to see your head teacher/walk right into her office) and note that Eric says something, which allows a fade.

- Radio is a great media for the use of imaginative and creative music. Radio plays start with appropriate music – even fifteen or twenty seconds of music can evoke a scene. Music can denote danger, joy or mystery. The trick is finding the right music to fit in with what is going on in the play. I always found my students up for this task! I am sure you will, too.
- In radio scripts, your students can let their imaginations run riot! They can invent their own two scenes for a radio play or use one of the following three plots.

  a) Winston Churchill's DNA is used (or President Kennedy's DNA). He has been recreated just as his country faces its biggest crisis since he was leader. How does Churchill (Kennedy) persuade his country that he needs to take charge as Prime Minister (President) immediately?
  b) Look again at the plot concerning Terry and the aliens. This could work better as a radio play. Rewrite and extend the plot and use it as a radio play.
  c) Poor rich girl Laura Stubbs has been kidnapped. She has been placed in the basement of a large house. She has three guards, one woman and two men. She will only be released if her rich oil tycoon father coughs up the large ransom.

Your students can write two or three scenes of their radio play and record them – using music, sound effects and fade-ins and outs at the appropriate places.

Scripting

Ask your students to script a film, a play suitable for television or a radio drama. They can work in groups of four or five.

Step One: Thought shower some ideas and bullet point the main events of the drama. For example, television drama.

- A gang decide to rob a post office but their plans are overheard by two teenagers.
- The teenagers are spotted by the gang leader, who is angry. The gang chase the teenagers into a blind alley.

- The teenagers are trapped but escape into a deserted and condemned tenement block.
- The teenagers are confronted by a tramp, who hides them down a disused lift shaft.
- The gang quiz and threaten the tramp but he claims he has not seen anyone in the tenement block.
- The teenagers escape and contact the police.
- The police refuse to believe the story at first. However, the tramp arrives at the station and confirms the story.
- The police arrive at the bank, just in time. The gang are arrested.

Step Two: The group will need to story board their ideas. When story boarding, artistic endeavour is not important. Match-stick figures will do! Underneath the drawings should be some brief dialogue.

Step Three: The group can look at the story board, suggest changes and script the piece – working from the bullet points and the story board.

Step Four: The group now need to read through the script and suggest changes.

Step Five: During this stage, the group can rehearse the piece, making small changes as necessary.

Step Six: The group can perform the piece in front of other groups. The watching group might suggest ways in how the script can be improved. They could possibly work from the following chart.

	Performance	Answer	Suggestions
Plot			
Voice			
Action			
Emotions			
Space			

Questions students might ask

Can we hear the actors? Does the story work? Is the plot sustained? Do the actors act well? Is there sufficient eye contact? Are hand gestures used? Do the emotions come across?

Is the acting space used effectively? Does tone of voice change?

Below is an example of a chart in action. Ask your students if they feel the chart is used effectively?

	Performance	Answer	Suggestions
Plot	Is the story a good one? Does it work? Is the storyline sustained?	Yes – except for the final scene. The final scene was poor.	The final scene degenerated into a fight. A complete re-write of the final scene would make the play believable.
Voice	Can we hear the actors?	Mostly.	Two of the group need to work on voice projection.
Actions	Is the play acted out effectively? Is eye contact good? How effective were hand gestures?	We could suspend disbelief. Yes. Fine – except for one actor.	No improvements necessary. One of the team kept his hands limply by his sides throughout the play – suggest he works on hand-gestures.
Emotions	Do the emotions come across?	Mostly.	The gang leader did not show his anger.
Space	Was the full acting space used?	Yes.	

Ask your students if they can add any categories to the chart? As watchers, can they use the chart for the plays they are viewing? Did the chart work?

CHAPTER 4

Elements of drama

Characterization

For successful characterization – to make the character believable – an actor needs the following–

1) To have thoroughly read the script or to have talked through the role play – so that he/she has a complete understanding of the role. In other words, an actor should ask him/herself;
    - Does my character evoke audience sympathy or hatred?
    - Is my character meant to be good, bad or neutral?
    - Does my character change throughout the play, or change at one dramatic point or remain the same throughout?
2) To stay in character (sustain the role).
    - The actor needs to make sure, for example, if (s)he needs to put on an accent – and if so, that accent needs to be maintained throughout the play.
3) The actor needs to be sure that the created character is believable. The actor needs to ask him/herself the following–
    - What is my character meant to look like?
    - What is my character's role in the play?
    - What are my character's motives in the play? Is the character meant to be kind, cruel or indifferent?
    - What does my character say?
    - What does my character do?
    - What do the other characters say about my character? Is there a difference between what they say about my character when he/she is onstage and when he/she is off stage?

- How do the other characters react to my character? Are they afraid of my character or do they mock my character? Do they appear to like, dislike or mock my character? Do some characters react differently to my character than others? Why?

Ask your students the following; Imagine you are auditioning for the part of Alex Grimwood in the play, 'Tyrant'. Look at the script closely and decide how you would play the part.

'Tyrant'

Grimwood: (*snarls*) You are a bunch of no hopes. How am I meant to lick you lot into shape?

(*silence – the group appear subdued*)

You are supposed to be a revolutionary army. Don't make me laugh! You're a bunch of wet rags! Fit? You lot couldn't cross the smallest mountain without picking up colds, blisters, bad backs. If you hope to survive in this war you will need to get fit and fast. Your aim is to stay alive. You need to learn how to survive. I'm going to teach you . . . this very morning! Any questions? Anyone want out?

(*silence*)

Right, get yourselves into some semblance of order while I sort out the equipment.

(*Grimwood marches briskly into the hut.*)

Garrett: (*indicating Grimwood's back*) He's a mean man.

Wells: Got a nasty temper, too.

Rowe: (*shaking his head*) Knew the man years ago. His bark's worse than his bite.

Garrett: (*annoyed*) Don't like the man!

Bland: (*speaking slowly*) You may not like the man, Garrett, but he'll lick you into shape and keep us all alive. He's a leader – and a leader has to lead!

Having read through the script, ask your students what they know about Grimwood. How should he be played? Now ask your students about the other characters. How should they be played? What do they say about Alex Grimwood? Which characters might move and speak with purpose? Which characters might make small hand gestures and which might use grand gestures? Which might use eye contact and to whom? Could some of the characters act, speak and move differently when with other characters?

Now ask your students to look at another scene from the same play.

'Tyrant'
Act Two Scene Two.
The rebels are camped near a mountain top They are under enemy fire. They are cold and hungry. Some are sick. All are weary.

Bland: (*to the group*) Alex Grimwood is a good man. He has a plan. He won't let us down.

Wells: Aye, he's got a plan alright. It's such a wonderful plan we're all *dying* to hear it.

Garrett: (*dispirited*) He's brought us all here to rot or to die by enemy bullets.

Rowe: (*coughs*) My lungs are bad.

Wells: We need a change of leader – do away with Grimwood. Keep him and we all die!

Bland: (*annoyed*) And you're the right man to take over, are you Wells? You chicken-livered coward, you haven't the guts to confront the man. Who's going to do away with Alex? *You?* Don't make me laugh!

Wells: Aye, well – perhaps I would, if he was here right now. I'd tell him what I think.

(*Grimwood storms into the camp*)

Grimwood: Right, you lot – we're ready to march.

(*The men stand to attention*)

Bland: (*to Wells*) Got something to say to the boss, Wells?

(*Wells shakes his head, Bland scoffs*)

Grimwood: Right, let's get moving.

Ask your students what they have learned from this episode. How do the men act towards Grimwood and to each other? How should each character be played? Which character's tone of voice could be deep? Is there a character who could have a high-pitched voice? Which character(s) might speak with firmness and authority and which might speak quickly and nervously?

Bringing characters to life

Ask your students to get into groups of five and act out the two scenes. Is there a moment in the dialogue when a gesture could be used – such as a finger to the lips or a warning gesture? Perhaps a tone of voice could be changed?

When thinking of developing characterization, a chart could be used such as the following;

	How might this help characterization?
Gestures	
Voice	
Movement	

Here is a completed chart, to use as an example.

	How might this help characterization?
Gestures	I could fold my arms and glare at the men. This would show I was disgusted with them.
Voice	I could snarl and bark out my orders. This would show I was in authority.
Movement	I could turn my back on the others. This would show that I was in control.

The emotions

Characters need to show their emotions. Students can find this quite difficult. Ask your students to try the following – concentrating on their facial expressions;

- In pairs, look as surprised as you possibly can. Imagine someone has told you that you have won first prize in a competition. When surprised, your eyes may become wider and the whites of your eyes should become more pronounced. Perhaps your eyebrows might become curved and raised.
- In pairs, look as frightened as you possibly can. Imagine you have seen a ghost and the ghost is floating towards you. Again you need to concentrate on facial expression. A frightened person might not look directly into another's eyes. Wrinkles may appear on their forehead.
- In pairs, and concentrating on your facial expression, display anger. An angry person's eyebrows will narrow and his/her eyes might appear to be 'popping out of their sockets'. Maybe their nostrils will flare. Perhaps you have spent hours on your homework project and your little brother has screwed it up. He is sitting on the floor laughing at the remains of your homework!
- Finally, in pairs, try looking as if you are feeling really sick. Perhaps you have smelt something bad or seen a decayed corpse of an animal. How will you look? Maybe your hand will cover your mouth or your eyes may protrude.

Thinking about voice

Characters speak in different ways. They may speak with 'a plum in their mouth' or with an accent or dialect. Ask your students to try speaking with a different accent to their own. Then ask them to speak deliberately slowly, then very quickly, then loudly and finally quietly – so that they can just be heard. Your students should notice that they can change a character depending upon accent and the way the lines are spoken.

Ask your students to look at the passage below and, in pairs, take turns speaking it in an accent different from their own. They can change their usual pace and volume to create a character that is not themselves!

> I'm here because I want to tell you something about my life. Did you know I was born here, in this village. I even attended the local school – and a few years' later the big school in town, although it wasn't a comprehensive in those days.
>
> My dad owned the local store in the high street. He wanted me to join him, to take over. But I couldn't – I wanted something bigger in my life. I decided to seek fame and fortune elsewhere. Well, you all know what happened to me . . . what became of me. I'm just giving you the minor details.
>
> You see me now and you can tell what became of me, by the way I speak and the clothes I wear.

Ask your students if they feel the character did find fame and fortune or not? The way the character speaks may betray the fact that the character did well in life, or not. Is the character male or female and does this matter?

Tell your students that changing the *movement* of the character might change our perspective of that character. Your students can try the following;

- Walk as a young person – briskly and with purpose.
- Walk as an older person – slowly and carefully.
- Walk with a limp.
- Skip and jump like a very young person.
- Walk as if the character is depressed – slump your shoulders and look at the ground.
- Walk as if your character is thinking deeply. Perhaps the character is rubbing their chin?
- Walk as if you are sick, perhaps one hand on your stomach.

Characters and jobs

Ask your students to mime the following, choosing just one of the following;

- An electrician
- A bank manager
- A waiter

- A taxi driver
- A doctor

Now ask your students to guess the job that is mimed. How did they guess? What was done that seemed obvious for the person's job?

Working in pairs, ask your students to act out an improvisation where two of the following meet. For example, an electrician might visit the bank manager to discuss his overdraft. Or the taxi driver might visit the doctor's surgery.

Rhythm

The rhythm of a drama means the speed in which the action moves. The speed can change during a performance – depending upon a particular circumstance. The rhythm (and tempo) is the concept of incorporating speed and intensity to physical actions. For instance, as humans we pace ourselves differently according to different given circumstances. We might enter a dentist's surgery slowly – knowing we are to undergo a particular treatment. However, we may walk as quickly as possible from the same surgery once treatment is complete – to get far away from the place where we experienced discomfort.

Your students need to think about how **real** people might behave in **real** situations. Ask them to look at the scenarios below and think about the rhythm of those following situations. Your students might like to work in pairs.

- Leaving school at the end of the summer term.
- Visiting a sick relative in hospital.
- Meeting their boy/girlfriend.
- Meeting their Head of Year because they are in trouble.
- Spotting a long lost friend from a distance.

Now ask your students to act out one or two of the scenarios and see if their walk can match the situations.

Rhythm can change with the circumstances. Ask your students to look at the scenarios again and allow the rhythm and tempo to change as the situation changes.

- Leaving school at the end of the summer term but your friend, who was feeling ill, suddenly collapses. What do you do?
- Visiting a sick relative only to find the bed empty and your relative gone!
- Meeting your girl/boy friend but they don't turn up and you walk home.

- Meeting your Head of Year but the meeting is cancelled and you can catch up with your friends instead.
- Spotting a long lost friend in the distance but as you get closer you realize that person just **looks** like your friend and is, in fact, a stranger!

A good play/improvisation might include different rhythms within one scene and certainly during a few scenes. For example;

Scene One: The main character is centre stage, in the spotlight, talking about his problems with the law. He speaks slowly but speeds up towards the end of that scene as he talks about his arrest.

(The rhythm of speech might start slowly but increase in tempo.)

Scene Two: A busy market place. The characters are stopping to look at goods and then rapidly moving on. Lines spoken by the actors might be one-liners or part of a speech –such as; 'Get out of my way,' or 'Excuse me . . . how much are the apples?' or 'Can I buy . . . ' The main character might be pickpocketing.

(The rhythm would be uneven and the tempo and pace of the scene would be quick.)

Scene Three: Police break into the main character's flat. There is a scuffle. He is arrested. The speech would be loud and erratic, such as 'Dale, over here.' 'What the . . . '. 'Got you!'

(The rhythm and tempo here would be fast to match the action.)

Ask your students to look at the three short scenes, improvise and act them out, noting the different rhythm and tempo in each scene. Now ask them to look at the short scene below. Can they spot the rhythm and tempo in that scene? Does the rhythm and tempo change during the course of the scene? Ask them to perform the scene, thinking about rhythm, pace and movement.

'Life As We Know It.' By Lucy Luckmore
Act One Scene Three.
(*Lisa and Cary are talking to Stewart and Paul as others enter the classroom.*)
Lisa: (*emphatic*) 'Tell her nothin' Nothin'!
Cary: (*upset*) Can't say nothin' . . . it's more lies. Lies, lies, lies. Always lies.
Stewart: Telling Mr Driver nothin' ain't lies.
Paul: (*firm*) It's all your fault, Stew.
(*Stewart grabs Paul by the shirt collar and shakes him.*)
Stewart: Who says it's my fault, eh? You? Are *you* gonna say it's my fault, mighty mouse?
(*Barry bangs into Stewart as he barges past to get to his desk.*)
Barry: (*to Stewart*) Sorry, Stew.

Stewart: (*aside*) You will be, moron! (*releases Paul*) Think about it, Paul.
Carry: (*tearful*) This whole thing sucks.
Paul: Yeah, it sucks.
Stewart: (*angrily throws a punch at Paul, it fails to connect*) If I get the blame, you're dead meat!
(*A scuffle ensues. Paul is struck on the nose. The class is in uproar when Mr Driver opens the door.*)
Mr Driver: (*shouts*) What's going on in here?
(*There is instant silence.*)
Stewart Beddard, Paul Mulvey – here! Now! This instant!
(*Paul and Stewart walk up to Mr Driver.*)
Well? Explain!
Stewart: It was nothing, Sir.
Paul: Just friendly banter, Sir.
Mr Driver: Friendly-fire more like. Wipe the blood from your nose, Mulvey. Ah, now that reminds me. I want to see you boys at break.
Paul: Yes, sir.
Stewart: Yes, sir.
Mr Driver: (*his eyes wander the classroom*) You, too Lisa Clery and you – Cary Lyon.

Forms

The form of a piece of drama means the structure in which the story is told. It is also the way in which the characters are portrayed and how the language and dialogue is used. When teaching drama, I always liked to take a form that is well known and give it a twist – to surprise and shock the audience. For example, I took Brothers Grimm fairy tales and gave them a modern setting and the viewpoint from a minor character. Or I took a well-known legend, such as William Tell, and made him useless with the bow and arrow – but somehow or other he still managed to split the apple rather than his son's head.

Ask your students to work in small groups. They need to research a well-known story and give it a twist. For example Robin Hood could become Robina Hood, a girl. Or Robin Hood could be portrayed as a baddie and his merry men could be a desperate bunch of drunkards (playing on the word merry) who attempt to rob the rich to fund their lifestyle. The play could be performed through dance, singing, poetry reading and acting – or through a chorus reciting the story.

Contrasts

When writing scripts, your students need to consider the use of contrasting ideas. This will add tension and excitement to their written work. Contrasting ideas might be noise to silence (or silence to noise). It could be the contrast of views between young and old people. Contrasts can be about things seen or heard on stage – such as sweet playing music and then a terrible high-pitched wine, or the cacophonous noise of witches attempting to sing. There could be a contrast in the play as a whole. Scenes may be set in a castle and then in a hovel or a cave.

Characters can also offer contrasts. A young boy, an old woman or a nobleman and a peasant would offer contrasts. **A dark alleyway** evoking fear and danger can then be contrasted to a house party where everyone is enjoying themselves. There can be a contrast in the spoken language. A Queen will speak in a different way than one of her commoners. Shakespeare used this kind of contrast in his plays. The commoners spoke and used words in a different way than the courtiers.

In pairs, ask your students to think about contrasts. A can shout out a word and B can think of a contrast. After B has thought of ten contrasts, roles can be reversed and A needs to think of the contrasts. Here are some examples;

Happy/unhappy
Tame/wild
Hungry/full
Poor/rich
New/old
Well/ill

Ask your students to look at the possible plot for a play and work out the contrasts.

A prince walks from his castle. He is singing a happy tune. He enters a dark forest but soon finds himself lost in the forest. He sees an old lady, who is mournfully singing a dirge. She is collecting wood near her half tumbled down cottage. He walks up to her and she hobbles towards him, leaning on her stick. He notices how old and leather-skinned her face looks. She notices his youth and his rosy cheeked complexion. He stretches and breathes in the healthy fresh air. She wheezes and shrinks into herself.

The prince speaks to the old woman using courtly language. She answers him with grunts, gasps and gestures. He flings his purple coat aside and helps her gather sticks. His white tunic is soon dirty and stained. She huddles into her ragged cloak and shivers.

Now ask your students to work in small groups and write a synopsis for a possible play. They should offer contrasts. If stuck, they can develop the prince/old woman theme.

Conventions

There are certain drama conventions that most audiences will know and understand. These are as follows;

The audience aside is when a character from the play speaks directly to the audience. The audience aside is briefer than a soliloquy. Shakespeare used this convention for his character Falstaff in the play Henry IV Part Two.

Act Five, Scene One. Falstaff does not want to fight the enemy. The Prince has just told him that he owes God a death. Falstaff (alone on stage) debates the use of 'honour' if one is killed in action.

> Falstaff: 'Tis not due yet; I would be loath to pay him before his day. What need I be so forward with him that calls not on me? Well, 'tis no matter; honour pricks me on. Yea, but how if honour prick me off when I come on? How then? Can honour set to a leg? No. Nor an arm? No. Or take away the grief of a wound? No. Honour hath no skill in surgery, then? No. What is honour? A word. What is in that word? Honour. What is that honour? Air. A trim reckoning! Who hath it? He that died o' Wednesday. Doth he feel it? No. Doth he hear it? No 'Tis insensible, then? Yea, to the dead. But will it not live with the living? No. Why? Detraction will not suffer it. Therefore I'll none of it. Honour is a mere scutcheon. And so ends my catechism.

Ask your students to practise this speech in pairs or small groups. How should this speech be delivered? If possible, allow your students to see clips of this speech from recent films.

Below is a modern example of an audience aside;

> Lady Quintana: (*to butler*) Fetch me my garments, Pinnegar.
> Butler: Yes, my lady (*aside to audience*) . . . those garments won't fit my fine lady soon. She's expecting and it isn't the Lord Quintana's child, I can tell you!
> Lady Quintana: (*impatient*) Hurry, hurry Pinnegar. I'm late already.
> Butler: Yes, my lady. (*aside*) Patience was never one of my lady's virtues.

- The use of the soliloquy – which is when a character speaks his or her thoughts alone . . . there is no other character on stage, or the character(s) on stage cannot hear the speaker. The character often (but not always) speaks directly to the audience when looking directly at the audience. A long soliloquy is sometimes called a monologue.

Here is an example from Shakespeare's play 'Othello'.

- Iago is plotting against Cassio and wants Othello to think Cassio is conducting an affair with his wife. Below, Iago is telling the audience how Cassio is treating Desdemona and how he, Iago, can use Cassio's courtesy to his own advantage by sowing seeds of mistrust in Othello's heart.

Iago: (*aside*) He takes her by the palm. Ay, well said, whisper. With as little a web as this I will ensnare as great a fly as Cassio. Ay, smile upon her, do; I will gyve thee in thine own courtship. You say true; 'tis so, indeed. If such tricks as these strip you out of your lieutenantry, it had been better you had not kiss'd your three fingers so oft, which now again you are most apt to play the sir in. Very good; well kissed! And excellent courtesy! 'Tis so, indeed. Yet again your fingers to your lips? Would they were clyster-pipes for your sake!

(In this case, Iago is speaking out his thoughts while observing Cassio and Desdemona.)

Here is a modern example;

Butler: (*soliloquy*) I used to dream of greater things. Dreams that are now dust – like the days of my life. Gone – like the money that's dripped through my thieving fingers. Spent, like my youth, on useless things . . . things of vanity. So now you see me in my dotage – working for that intolerant and intolerable Lady Quintana. I should be surrounded by grandchildren, loved by my kith and kin. I'm an outcast, condemned to servitude until I drop. I lied about my virtuous lady, too. What can be done? Oh, what can be done!

Ask your students to write a soliloquy for Lady Quintana, mentioning her useless and thieving butler who is prone to lies and exaggerations.

- Space – part of the stage (or acting area) can be established as one location and a different part (or different parts) can be used for different locations. For example;

Centre stage right	Centre stage left
The railway carriage.	Miss Miller's classroom.

Down Stage Centre
Jen's bedroom.

Ask your students to work out an improvisation where they might need two or three locations on stage at the same time. If stuck, they can use the example and work out an improvisation around the three acting areas in the example above.

- **Slow motion** – to show something that happened quickly – but could not happen so quickly on stage. For example, a train crash.

Symbols (2)

We have looked at symbols on page 44. A symbol can represent a theme or an idea in drama. The symbols used are often well-known symbols that the audience will instantly understand. These might include–

- Costume – a white dress will represent purity, as in the convention of a white wedding dress.
- Props – a torn wedding photograph will represent separation through death or divorce.
- Character expressions – raised eyebrows might register surprise or disapproval.
- Gestures – a finger to the lips will be a symbol of requesting silence.

CHAPTER 5

Drama as a medium

Mime

Explain to your students that mime is a dramatic and creative expression **without** the use of words. If possible, give them snippets of a silent movie.

Tell your students that mime is usually like acting in that it is a dramatic composition involving at least one character, a conflict, a theme and a story with a resolution. It is often thought of as silent acting – early films used mime.

Today, mime has a style of its own. It was originally used as a part of formal theatre in the orient. The Greeks took up mime for their drama and often used mime with dance.

In Britain, church drama used a form of mime in its miracle plays.

There are two well-known forms of mime today. One is *literal* mime, which tells a story with a conflict. This uses a main character and the actions of that character (or characters) tell a story. The other is *abstract* mime. This is used to explore feelings, thoughts and images through a topic or an issue. In this form of mime, there is no plot or main character.

Ask your students to mime one of the three following actions.

Individual Mime 1) Getting ready
- Looking at the clock.
- Running a shower or bath.
- Taking the shower/bath.
- Drying oneself.
- Finding clothes.
- Getting dressed.

- Looking for wallet/purse.
- Checking clock again, shaking head.
- Running for the bus/train or taxi.

Individual Mime 2) At the restaurant
- Entering the restaurant.
- Looking for a table.
- Sitting at the table.
- Summoning the waiter (perhaps using a hand gesture).
- Waiting for the food to arrive.
- Sniffing the food.
- Eating the food.
- Drinking.
- Leaving the restaurant.

Individual Mime 3) The car won't start
- Sitting in the car.
- Turning the ignition.
- Getting out of the car, opening the bonnet.
- Checking the engine.
- Unscrewing the oil cap.
- Using the dipstick.
- Showing annoyance with car.
- Trying the ignition again.
- Locking and leaving the car.

Group mime

In small groups, your students can try one of the two following options;

- A comedy sketch – where a person goes into a shop to buy a suit. The person needs measuring for the suit. When the suit arrives, it does not fit! The action is repeated twice more, except the person measuring for the suit changes. Eventually, the customer tramples on the suit and walks out of the shop.
- A person enters a doctor's surgery. That person feels itchy and scratches his/her hair and body. The person appears to be trying to catch hold of something. The next person at the surgery begins to feel itchy and scratches his/her body . . . and so on. The final person catches hold of a flea and returns it to the first person!

Emotions (2)

Working in groups, your students can mime out an emotion or emotions that have a theme. Below is an example;

The theme is displayed in the background and in the case of this example, it is a warning against drink-driving.

- Students mime staggering with imaginary cans in their hands. They display characteristics of binge drinkers. They wear paper hats and their clothes are dishevelled. (enjoyment/ irresponsibility)
- Two students emerge from imaginary cars. They argue and gesticulate at their damaged cars. (anger)
- A parent (or parents) are at the bedside of an injured child. (worry/care)
- A lone figure, holding flowers stoops down at an imaginary graveside. (dejection/sorrow)

Costume

Introduction

In a school production, or when your students are performing in front of others, costume can be used to enhance mood. Costume can help to identify groups of characters; such as priests, soldiers or groups of people (dress Montagues, in *Romeo and Juliet*, for example, in one colour and Capulets in another).

Costume can also assist a plot. For instance, a character might change during the course of a play. Costume can show that a particular character is growing up (Pip in a play version of 'Great Expectations' or David in a play version of 'David Copperfield') – or show a change in fortune, from rags to riches or riches to rags.

Costume can indicate mood, theme or issues.

If used successfully, costume can communicate meaning, character and theme. It can also link in with lighting, make-up and props to give, for example, a Victorian theme.

Ask your students to think of appropriate costume for a play you are studying in drama or that they might have studied in English, for example, Gerald Croft ('An Inspector Calls') or Rita ('Educating Rita). For younger students, choose a character from a book they may have studied in English – for example, Salom ('Tribes') or Damian ('Millions'). Your students can draw the costume appropriate for the character in the book or play.

1) Simple costume

It is important to think about time and cost when considering costume. In a school situation, simple but effective costume can be the best option. There are two ways to deal with simple costume–

- Dress everyone in a dark colour with some appropriate props.

- Dress everyone in a different colour and make the colour symbolic as to character. For example, a fiery-tempered character could be dressed in red.

If you go for the first option, your students could wear a different sash or wristband for character identification purposes.

Masks

Your students may well enjoy making their own masks or using masks to create their character. Masks can be used to show a particular emotion – such as sadness. They can also be used to show a trait, such as gluttony. Ask your students what might a mask look like that shows sadness? What might a mask look like that shows gluttony?

Tell your students that in theatre, masks can be used as disguise. Perhaps a character wishes to keep his/her identity a secret from another character for some reason.

Masks can also be a way of representing action in a different way. For instance, death or the passing of the seasons can be shown through wearing masks. Often, this type of action can be shown through mime and/or dance. Ask your students if they can design masks representing the different seasons.

Actors will sometimes use masks when storytelling. This is especially true if the story is depicting supernatural or magical events.

Finally, if an actor or actors take on a number of roles (identities) in a play, they may well use masks. In modern times, when using a large cast will cost a theatre company too much money, this reason for using masks has gained in popularity.

1) *How to make a mask*
If you decide that your students could make up their own masks, you will need the following;

- A sheet of paper
- A pencil
- Scissors
- Heavy cardboard
- Brightly coloured felts
- Elastic
    1) Ask your students to decide on making up their own character. They will need to design their own mask shapes. They can draw their mask shapes on a sheet of copy paper. The mask needs to cover their whole face.
    2) Now they will need to draw a circle for the eyes and a nose bridge.

3) Using scissors, they will need to cut out the mask shape, the space for their eyes to see through, and the two parallel lines for the nose bridge.

4) Your students can check that the mask covers their face before proceeding further. I have found, at this point, some students need to repeat this part of the exercise!

5) Now your students can trace the mask shape onto a piece of cardboard, for some groups it might be easier if they used glue to stick the paper carefully onto the cardboard.

6) Your students now need to carefully cut out the eyeholes and then cut two tiny holes in the two far corners of the mask. They then insert the elastic, tying the elastic so that it won't slip out. They may want to slip the mask over their heads to check the elastic is not too tight.

7) Finally, allow your students to colour their masks and decorate as appropriate. Some students I have taught have taken the masks home and decorated them by sticking beads to the masks, or adding wool for hair.

Health and safety warning: Tell your students that they must never place their scissors near their face when trying the positions of the eye holes.

2) *A brief history of masks in theatre*
Tell your students the following information;

The Ancient Greeks used masks to honour or worship their mytho- logical gods. The masks were oversized and exaggerated. They were often fitted around the mouth, so that the actors could project their voices during a performance.

During the middle ages, mystery plays were performed. Masks were used to dramatize the characters. Mystery plays were mostly written by church priests and the masks were used to show the ugliness of sin. The masks were grotesque and often portrayed Satan or one of the seven deadly sins.

In the fifteenth century the Italian art 'Commedia Dell Arte' was formed. Characters were used in a particular plot, so that people became familiar with the characters and the plot. The plot consisted of two rich characters who wanted to arrange a marriage between their children to protect their fortunes. One of the children is in love with a poorer character. The lovers feel their love is doomed. After a series of problems, the young lovers defy their parents and are able to marry – the servants who helped them receive a reward and the rich older people are deceived. Well-known stock characters (wearing stock masks) are Pantalone – a rich merchant and his rich merchant friend, Cassandro. Another well-known character is Brighella – the sly butler. (See www.marskmaker.dk/eng/commediadellarte.htm)

Noh Theatre masks are used in Japan. Each mask in Noh Theatre represents a certain type of person – perhaps a hero, a devil, a ghost or a legendary animal.

Noh Theatre masks have been used in Japan for over five thousand years. The Japanese masks were made out of clay or wood. They covered the whole face.

3) *How to make a clay mask*
If your students have the opportunity of making a clay mask, you will need the following;

- Clay
- A blank piece of paper, to cover the whole face
- Paint
- A sculpting knife tool
- A sculpting needle tool
- A rolling pin
- Elastic
  1) Your students will need to use a rolling pin and roll out a large slab of clay, about ¼ inch thick.
  2) They will need to work out the shape of the mask, making sure it will fit their face. To do this, they can make a blank paper mask and then place the clay thickly around the inside of the paper mask.
  3) They can cut away the excess clay from around the mask by using a sculpting knife tool.
  4) Your students will then need to cut out some eye and nose holes, from the mask. They need to make sure they have enough breathing space – as the masks need to be worn over the face!
  5) They can add or cut the clay away until they are happy with the mask shape. They then need to use the sculpting needle tool to insert two holes for the elastic to go through.
  6) Your students then need to leave the mask so that it will dry out before removing the paper from the mask.
  7) After a week, the masks will be dry enough to go into the ceramic kiln.
  8) Once fired, the masks can be painted in colours or patterns – the elastic put in and secured and the masks worn!

Tip: Liaise with the art department for use of the sculpting tools and for use of the ceramic kiln. Different clays have different firing times – so if possible know the type of clay you are dealing with and seek art department advice!

4) *What to do with the masks*

In small groups, your students can use their masks for one of the following three improvisations;

- Imagine you are writing a modern mystery play about binge drinking. Use masks for the binge drinkers and different masks for the victims of binge drinking – or the police.
- The animals are rebelling against human rule. They manage to escape and find their way into a forest. The humans can wear one type of mask, to depict them as cruel owners. The animal masks can each represent a different type of animal.
- A spaceship has landed on a new planet. There are two different types of creatures on the planet – hostiles and friends. The two distinct types can wear different masks. The space explorers can wear a third type of mask.

Make-up

Tell your students that make-up is the use of cosmetic paint, various powders and colouring. These are used to make face paints visible to the audience. Make-up artists often liaise with lighting crews to make sure the overall effect of make-up and lighting is right in order to create a particular mood or atmosphere.

The use of make-up depends upon the type of play that is to be acted out. If the play uses aliens or creatures from Greek mythology, make-up might be lavish. If the play is placed in a modern setting, then make-up may be at a minimum – to give a natural look.

Ask your students how they would make-up the following characters;

- An elf from a deep forest
- An Ork – evil and intent on destruction
- A vampire
- An explorer who has just returned from the desert
- A modern policeman

Tip: Remember the students are thinking about make-up rather than costume.

1) *Why use make-up?*

When acting on stage, it is important that your students' features can be clearly seen by everyone watching – including the back row!

Young people do not usually need heavy make-up, unless their characters are animals or fantasy figures.

Here are the stages necessary for make-up.

1) Your students need to wash their faces thoroughly with soap or face cleanser.
2) They need to apply an even coat of foundation over the whole face – blending into the neck.
3) Once the foundation is applied, use lighter and darker foundation to emphasize or create highlights and shadows.
4) Use colour on the cheeks and lips as stage lights can 'bleach out' the face.
5) If your students are playing an older person (for example) they might need special attention. They should look at pictures of older people to see where the skin has wrinkled and sagged. Your student might need to smile, frown and see where the skin would naturally wrinkle. Then a brown eyeliner pencil should be applied to draw into the wrinkles.
6) For plays set in the past, different make-up needs are necessary. In some periods of history, men and women have powdered their faces white, painted their lips red and drawn beauty marks onto their faces!
7) Special effects can be visible by an intelligent use of make-up. Latex and spirit gum can make scars, wounds or crooked noses.
8) Liner pencils should be used to make a student's eyebrows visible. Carefully stroke a little colour into the hair – not too much. Usually you just need to gradually darken the hairs.
9) Eyes need to look big but sometimes they will benefit from a small touch of mascara or eyeliner. For some plays, female students might need false eyelashes.
10) Eyelids and cheeks might need pressed powder colours. If you need a natural look, use matt finishes only. A highlight can lift shadows on the eye, a shadow several shades below the foundation colour will accentuate the socket line and a rouge can add touches of warmth to the foundation.

2) *Items you need*

- Hair brushes – an eyeliner brush to apply cake eyeliner. A lip brush, a rough/blusher brush, a powder brush, for dusting off excess powder, a socket brush – for shading into the socket line and two ¼ inch contour brushes, to apply eyeliner and shadow. Finally, a velour powder puff to fix the matt oil-based foundations.

- You can buy anti-shine creams and powders for matting the skin, when you apply very little make-up.
- Tooth enamel, coming in various colours, can be used for special effect. For example, if you wish to create a vampire with red fangs!

Tip: If you are running a school production, don't try and do everything yourself. When I ran school productions, I always got in somebody to do the make-up with the help of non-acting volunteer students. It takes away some of the pressure and means you can concentrate on the acting side of the production.

Ask your students to return to the activity where they suggested make-up for the elf, the ork, the vampire, the explorer and the policeman. In small groups, ask them to take it in turns to make-up those characters for a theatre production. You will need a make-up kit!

Music (2)

I have mentioned the use of music previously (page 42). It is worth reminding students that music can create and evoke atmosphere. Music can allow the scenes to flow and introduce and end plays and improvisations. It is imperative that your students do not allow **background** music to drown out the actors' voices. Actors need to be heard!

Students are very good at choosing the correct music for a drama piece. However, show them how different types of music can change mood and atmosphere. For example, loud music from a heavy metal band would convey a different mood from mournful violin playing.

Ask your students to look at the following script and decide on what music can be used and when–

Young Again

An old man is playing a mournful tune on his violin. He stops playing and
   listens to the birds chirping in the trees.

Old Oswald: *(signs)* Ah, if only I could have all that I've lost.

Elf: *(pops up from behind a tree)* What have you lost, old man?

Old Oswald: Why, I've lost the most precious thing – I've lost my youth.
   I'd do anything to be young again.

Elf: Then you shall be young again!

*(The old man hears sweet music playing in the distance. He walks towards
   the music. He is next seen standing outside a market square. He is now
   young again. There are sounds of buying and selling and joyful music in
   the air. He can hear the sound of happy laughter.)*

Oswald: *(shouts out loud)* I can't believe it . . . I'm young again!

*(Oswald dances to the music. The music suddenly stops to be replaced by
   a royal fanfare as the King and his daughter approaches.)*

King: *(to his daughter)* Who is that young man dancing in the market square?

Ask your students to read through the script and decide what music is required and to decide when it is needed. They will need to find the following;

- Violin music, unless one of them can play the violin
- Sweet music
- Joyful music

Now ask them to find the appropriate music as a homework piece. They can then improvise the scene using the appropriate music.

Sound effects

If your students read through 'Young Again' they will notice further sound cues, such as 'birds chirp in the trees.' These sound cues need cue sheets.

Sometimes microphones are necessary. You might need to invest in one for musicals, or liaise with your music department. This sort of equipment is changing as technology changes. It is better to go for a dearer microphone than one which might be considered cheap and nasty.

At present, an actor's mouth will need to be near the microphone – however, some high-quality microphones can pick up your students' voices if you hang them over the acting area. If your student is singing a solo, it is better to use a radio throat microphone. These microphones are clipped to the student's clothing, near to the throat. The microphone is picked up by a transmitter, which plugs into the mains and a control desk. It is worthwhile seeing what equipment your school has and work with that equipment!

If your student is using a hand-held microphone, you should use a sponge to cover the part of the microphone nearest the mouth. This ensures the quality of the sound by eliminating unwanted noises.

Tip: Avoid high-pitched feedback by placing your speakers as far down stage as possible.

Using school equipment as far as possible, ask your students to try using music technology. They can script a musical piece, perhaps writing their own songs – or use well-known songs. They can try using microphones to go with their musical piece. If they do write their own songs, they might wish to turn 'Young Again' into a musical. If so, they will need to write songs appropriate for the script.

Lighting

When I put on my first production, the technology teacher (also in charge of lighting for my version of 'Tom Sawyer') told me it is much better to have too much light than too little. I still believe he was right.

The specialist lights are called lanterns. They are used to focus the audience on a particular part of the acting area or on the whole stage. Lights can fade in and out for effect and they can add colour for effect. Remember, technology is changing very quickly. As I understand it, most schools are behind with technology (certainly the schools I taught drama in were behind!) and, at present, the ideas below are appropriate for most schools.

As a play starts, lights usually fade in. The action should start before lights are fully up. As a scene ends, lights usually fade out. As they fade out, the actors can create a freeze-frame picture to stick in the minds of an audience.

Lighting can be used for the following reasons;

- To gain an audience' attention to an important part of the stage at any given moment. Or it can draw the audience' attention to specific scenery, such as the hangman's noose.
- To promote a particular mood. A deep blue light will create a cold mood but a brighter red light might give a healthy rosy look to the scene.
- Lighting can be used to indicate a change in plot or action – for example a new character might be brought in and have a spotlight focus – such as the hangman! Action can shift from one part of the stage to another through the use of the spotlight. Or the focus can shift from one character to another through the use of a spotlight.
- An indication of time change can be achieved through lighting. Daytime to night time or night time to daytime.

If possible, allow your students to experiment with lighting – perhaps using an improvised piece they have already written when working through this book.

Your light

Students should note that it is important to find their light when acting. They should know where to stand at the right time. For example, a spotlight might be rose coloured so that a particular atmosphere is gained. The student will need to find the exact spot to take full effect of the lighting technique. Your student could draw a chalk cross on the part of the stage where that student will sing a solo – so that the student is right under the spot light!

Thoughts when producing a play
Houselights

The houselights are the ordinary lights in the theatre or drama studio. Just before the drama starts, it's a good idea to dim these lights, so that a sense of anticipation is gained.

Strobe lighting

Sometimes you may wish to use strobe lighting, which gives the effect of making the action appear slow. This use of strobe lighting can be very effective for use in fight scenes (Montague servants and Capulet servants in 'Romeo and Juliet' for example) or in frantic action such as survivors escaping a ship wreck.

A word of warning: If strobe lighting is used, the audience need to be aware. Strobe lighting can bring on epileptic fits. It should be used sparingly!

Uplifting

Lighting the actors from below can create a large shadow. This can be effective for a particular scene – when an evil character is about to murder another. This technique has been used in old black and white films and for melodrama. It builds up tension.

Tip: As with make-up, if you are working on a school production, it is a good idea to appoint an adult volunteer to take control of lighting. In my experience of school productions, I have always found somebody who (with the help of students) has been able to take charge of lighting.

Ask your students to look at the scene below and mark in where they would place the lighting. Is there anywhere they could use spotlights? Could floodlights be used? Can uplifting help the plot?

Ask your students to work in groups of about four or five and read the following script:

'Mercy Beckensale – A Victorian Girl'

Act One Scene One

(Mercy is standing alone, front stage. It is very early morning. The birds are singing in the trees.)

Mercy: Here I am, driven from the home I was born in, driven from the village I've lived in all my life. This is because they think I stole from the Countess. *(She stifles a sob)* It was all a lie, I tell you. A rotten lie! I stole nothing. Want to know the truth? See what happens.

(Nightime. Countess Radcliff's study.)

Do you see a dark shadow? It's Oliver Folkson. Take note. Look what he's doing.

Oliver: *(stoops)* Ah, a casket of jewels to last me a lifetime. Think I'll emi-grate to the New World. Make my fortune? Ha ha, I'll start a new life with a fortune!

(He places the jewels in his pocket, but one spills onto the table. Soon, it is daylight.)

Maid: *(cries)* Countess, Countess. Your jewels are nearly all gone. A thief has been here!

Countess *(walking briskly into the study)* What are you talking about girl?

Maid: Look, your casket is empty. Most of the jewels are missing!

Countess: *(thinking)* I know who's done this! That half-gypsy girl will be to blame – Mercy Beckensale. Wasn't she in this very study yesterday afternoon? Wanted to see me, complaining about something or other!

(Mercy is once again front-stage)

Mercy: *(to the audience)* So you see why they blamed me? Half-gypsy – that means half-**other** . . . something they can't understand. What am I to do? How can I bring that Oliver Folkson to justice? How can I redeem my name?

Having read through the script, your students now need to add in the lighting.

Props and sets

Properties

Properties are the items used by actors during a performance. They can be carried on stage by an actor – these properties might include a gun or a sword. Properties can also be added to a set before a particular scene – this could include a telephone or a bomb.

If you are involved in a school production, it is a good idea to appoint a properties supervisor. It is essential that the actor carries the right props for a particular scene or that the right prop is in the right place, on the correct set, for a particular scene. Performance disasters can strike if props are missed. For example:

Magician: *(to servant)* Fetch me my cloak!
Servant: Where is your cloak, oh famous one?
Magician: Behind the chair, you fool of a servant.
Servant: *(notices the prop is missing)* Er, um – oh no it isn't!

(At this point the property manager breaks out in a sweat and orders a student to throw the cloak onto the stage, which raises an unintentional laugh among the audience and ruins a crucial and serious scene.)

The property supervisor (with student volunteer help) will need to collect all the properties and check they are where they should be for a performance. The property supervisor needs to devise a sheet before the production. To get your students used to property sheets, allow them to use a simplified version before any improvisation work.

 Property Sheet (example)
Production: 'Mercy Beckensale – A Victorian Girl'

Properties needed	Where from?	Collected?
Mop and bucket	School caretaker	Given on night of performance
Cradle	Mrs Kemp (Gina Kemp's mum)	Yes
Violin	Miss Morgan (music department)	Yes
Pipe	?	No

(And so on!) Your property sheet might need to show about fifty items for a full production.

Notice that a pipe has not been found. When somebody volunteers a pipe, the form is altered and the 'where from?' and 'collected?' sections are changed accordingly.

Tip: When the property is in, it is a good idea to place it in bundles with labels showing what scene(s) each property is needed for. This saves a frantic hunt on the night!

When you have collected all the properties in, run through the play as a properties rehearsal to make sure some of the students are comfortable with the properties and to check that nothing has been overlooked. It is no good, on the morning of the performance, to wonder why Alice is not holding a horse saddle but thin air!

Your properties manager will need a properties sheet to work on during the night of the performance. This is a different sheet to the one above. It is called a stage property sheet.

Stage Property Sheet (example)

Property	Act	Page	Position
Victorian books	1	9	Stage right, on desk
Pipe	1	11	On table, centre stage
Jewels and jewel casket	1	14	Stage left

(And so on . . .). For a large performance, you might want a property sheet for each act or each scene. If you rely on the above property sheet, it might look too long and run into several sheets anyway.

Below is an example of a *Stage Property Sheet* for each scene.

Stage Property Sheet. Act One Scene One (example)

Property	Page	Position
Victorian books	9	Stage right, on desk
Pipe	11	On table, centre stage
Jewels and jewel casket	14	Stage left

(And so on–). The page reference indicates the appropriate page in the script!

The properties manager will also need a properties sheet for each acting student. Encourage your students to remember what properties they will need for each scene. However, it is a good idea to check each student's property needs against a personal property sheet.

Personal Property Sheet (example)
Name: Annabella Plover
Character's Name: Mary Beckonsale

Property	Act	Page
Flower basket	1	2
Cloak	1	5
Broken shoe	1	10
Chain	2	4

(And so on–)

Sets

Sets can be complicated or simple. They can also change during a performance. Sometimes sets can change after every scene or they may only change at the start of each act.

For work in the drama room, it is easier to keep sets to the minimum. You can invest in interlocking rostra to create different levels for your students to work on.

Rostra blocks are easier to work with than chairs – they are also much safer.

For performances – such as a school production – you might need to invest in a *box set*. This can be made to look like part of a room. The sides and back are usually flat. Box sets are basically wooden frames with canvas stretched across them. You can then paint the canvas to any design and in any colour you wish. Box sets can be stored and reused. I was fortunate when directing my first school production because the technology department made the box sets for me and the art department painted the sets to my specification – all for free! I recommend that you liaise with the technology and art department, to see what they have time to do for you.

The box set flats can be joined together in order to create a full box set – such as a bedroom or a dining room. Box sets can be designed to have doors that can open, for entrance and exit purposes. Windows can be painted onto the box set flats, with a dark or light background outside-the-window view to denote night or day.

When I produced my own school play, 'Jason Brent', the technology department constructed a swivel box set. The swivel box set is reversible and is wonderful for quick scene change overs – these were essential for this particular play.

Types of sets

For some plays, you might want a *realistic* set. Perhaps a study, or a restaurant. For other plays, you might require a *stylized* set that helps to create an atmosphere corresponding to the themes of a play. There are five staging possibilities;

> **End On** – for this staging possibility, you might use a traditional stage in the school hall. The audience will be looking up at the acting area.
>
> **Thrust** – this is often more appropriate for a drama room. In this case, you have a middle acting area and the audience is sitting on three sides of the acting area. Some modern theatres have adapted this approach.
>
> **Traverse** – in this possibility, the audience is on both sides of the acting area but not directly in front of the acting area.
>
> **The Round** – the acting area, as the name suggests, is round and the audience 'surrounds' the acting area. The audience is, in effect, on every side. The idea is popular with small theatres and often used in the drama room, where there is limited space.
>
> **Promenade** – the audience is able to follow the actors from area to area. Stage sets are usually non-existent. This style is used by many outdoor productions, although I saw an excellent performance of 'The Tempest' using different parts of a castle for outdoor and indoor scenes. The audience was taken from one location to another by Ariel, the spirit.

Ask your students to talk about the advantages and disadvantages of each staging possibility.

The stage manager

For school productions I always appoint a stage manager. I remember my first attempt at producing a play. I thought I could do without a stage manager and things soon went wrong! Then, one lunch time, somebody in the staffroom came up and told me I needed a stage manager and he was volunteering. I quickly realized I could not do without him.

The stage manager holds the technical aspect of the performance together. He/she is the glue! The stage manager will consult with the designers of the sets and report to the director (you) as to how everything is progressing. As well as checking set design, a good stage manager will liaise with those working on costumes, properties and sound. This leaves you free to consult with just the stage manager – you can get on with making sure your students are learning their lines, speaking loudly enough and keeping on task . . . no small feat!

The stage manager should have a sets sheet – so that he/she knows when scenes change and that all the sets are ready and in place.

Sets Sheet (Example)

Set	Act/Scene		Position
Forest glade	1	1	Back and sides
Cave	1	2, 3, 4	Back and sides
Kitchen	2	1	Back. Table and 4 chairs, centre stage

(And so on . . .)

Staging terms

It is easier (to make sure everything is in the right place) for everyone to know staging terms. When I first directed school productions, I had to go on stage and physically show students where to stand or show the stage manager where I required the props, stage sets and speakers. I quickly decided that it was easier in the long run to use and explain staging terms. I could then show, on a diagram, where I wanted everything to go for a particular scene. Thus I avoided walking onto the staging area. In a school situation, the technology teacher, the art teacher and the teacher in-charge of props were all more likely to be found in the staffroom at break. It was easier showing them a diagram and explaining where I wanted what over a cup of coffee than asking them to meet me on stage in the school hall! It is worthwhile knowing the staging terms below;

Stage Positions (End on)

Upstage Right	**Upstage Centre**	**Upstage Left**
Centre Stage Right	**Centre Stage**	**Centre Stage Left**
Down Stage Right	**Down Stage Centre**	**Down Stage Left**
	Audience	

Do note that left and right are always shown from the actor's point of view when on stage and when facing the audience.

CHAPTER 6

Working together

Improvisation

This is a good way of getting students used to the idea of working together. Improvisation techniques and ideas for improvisation are used throughout this book, however for one or two quick ideas, look back to pages 7, 8 and 9. Below are some further ideas, to get your students thinking.

1) *Role on paper*

Draw the outline of a human figure on a large piece of paper. Add details about the characters and allow your students to add their own ideas concerning this character. If stuck, your students could look at the character below!

He can't always think clearly
He acts on impulse
He lives with his mum
Has two younger brothers
Is a bully at school

Always in trouble   Has a pet dog
Hates lessons   Treats his pet well
Often skips school   Takes dog to training classes

Wants a job working with animals

Has few friends   Gets on with drama teacher
Listens to his granddad   Is small but well-built
Wants to find and meet his dad   Wants to own and drive a motorbike

Now ask your students to split into pairs and draw another character, adding in a profile for that person . . . taking care to use negative and positive sentences. Then, allow the characters to meet and improvise a scenario. Your students will need to name the characters. For example, the boy could meet one of the following people;

Boy/Drama teacher
Boy/Head of Year
Boy /Policeman
Boy/Dad
Boy/ Motorbike dealer
Boy/Vet

2) *Lines/no lines*

In pairs, your students need to imagine they are about to act out a scene in a play. However, one of the actors has bumped heads while changing and has completely forgotten his/her lines. However, the actor can improvise! The other actor knows the lines to the play word perfectly. One of the pair delivers the lines, the other needs to make them up! The audience are expecting a first-rate play!

You can use the lines of a play, where there are two actors on stage, or use my suggestions below.

Grave digger: There's a great person about to lie here. What was he . . . a well-known . . .
Vicar:
Grave digger: You're the Vicar, what are you going to say about him?
Vicar:
Grave digger: What'll you do after the funeral?
Vicar:

Here are two responses:

1) Evie's response
Grave digger: There's a great person about to lie here. What was he . . . a well-known . . .
Vicar: *A well-known poet.*
Grave digger: You're the Vicar, what are you going to say about him?
Vicar: *I'll tell them what a wonderful poet he was and how his books sold to millions.*
Grave digger: What'll you do after the funeral?
Vicar: *Oh, I'll go home and write Sunday's sermon.*

2) Savita's response
Grave digger: There's a great person about to lie here. What was he . . . a well-known . . .
Vicar: *You know very well he was a drunkard and a fool, despised by all!*

Grave digger: You're the Vicar, what are you going to say about him?

Vicar: *I haven't a clue. Any ideas? What do you say about such a man?*

Grave digger: What'll you do after the funeral?

Vicar: *Do the same as you; have a few pints and sleep it off.*

Here is a further improvisation for lines/no lines. The pair could work on this and then reverse, so both students have a go at improvising.

(*Dad and Dave enter the stage arguing.*)

Dad: I've told you, Dave, I'm not made of money.

Dave:

Dad: Don't pester me! Just go through that idea again.

Dave:

Dad: That's a ridiculous idea. Whatever will you come up with next?

Dave:

Dad: No, I can't accept that!

Dave:

Dad: And what did I hear about you this morning? Come clean, tell me everything!

Dave:

Dad: But you still haven't told me why the school phoned.

Your students can add to the storyline and put in some stage directions, as Connor and Dai have done, below.

Dad: (*annoyed*) I've told you, Dave, I'm not made of money.

Dave: (*sarcastic*) Oh, really? I thought you were the Bank of Dad. But I need the dosh . . .

Dad: Don't pester me! Just go through that idea again.

Dave: What, the one where I buy in a male guinea pig and we breed them and sell the babies?

Dad: That's a ridiculous idea. Whatever will you come up with next?

(*Dave paces around the room.*)

Dave (*enthusiastic*) We buy in a load of porridge oats, I make vats of porridge and we sell it outside the front door.

Dad: No, I can't accept that!

(*Dad sits on a kitchen chair and fiddles with the pepper pot.*)

Dave: You won't back any of my money spinners. Dad, you're a bore!

Dad: (*changing the subject*) And what did I hear about you this morning? Come clean, tell me everything!

Dave: I upset mum because I dropped out of the school play.

Dad: But you still haven't told me why the school phoned.

Dave: (*quickly*) Yes, well, I got myself into a little local problem.

Dad: (*suspicious*) Meaning what?

Dave: I forgot my maths homework . . . three weeks on the run.

Dad: You can forget borrowing money from me until you can organize yourself!

Dave: But dad . . .

A further improvisation you can use with your students is **ACE** – action/colour/emotion. Ask your students to start a story. Tell them that at any point in the story, another student (or you) can interrupt and ask for more detail about a particular event (action) or ask them what the colours were like in that scene. Was the car a red or blue one, for example? Or a student could be asked how he/she, or the protagonist, felt in a situation (emotion) and at a particular point. This forces the storyteller to think quickly. If a student group is shy or does not understand exactly what to do, you can become the storyteller and ask them to interrupt you.

Interviewing

Ask your students to work in pairs and imagine one of them is a famous musician, writer or film star. After about five minutes, ask them to reverse roles. Here is an example;

Nadini: I'm happy to meet and interview the famous Rory Wiltshire.
Rory: Yep, and my band are really going places.
Nadini: So, how did it all begin, Rory? How old where you when you knew you wanted to be a pop star?
Rory: (*thinking*) I bought my first guitar when I was five. My uncle taught me how to play . . . the chords and all that!
Nadini: When did the band come together?
Rory: We were all school mates . . . we lived in the same street. We used the shed and . . .
Nadini: (*interrupts*) The shed?
Rory: Yeah, my mate Sam lived in this tumbled-down house which had a large garden. There was this old rotten shed at the bottom of the garden. His dad had a few rusty spades in there. So we'd go into the shed with our acoustic guitars and work on a few songs I'd written.

As a variation, another pair might ask some questions, so that Rory will need to improvise quickly. For example:

Paul: What's the band called?
Rory: The Roaring Foxes.
Christine: Why?
Rory: Well, I like playing with words. Roaring is a dynamic word, full of energy. Down at the shed, we could smell foxes. Sometimes we'd see them. So, 'Roaring Foxes' sounded good.
Paul: Where did you hold your first gig?
Rory: In the school hall, just before Christmas, three years ago.

After some practice, your students should be able to work quickly on improvised scenes.

Concentration

It goes without saying that drama is a subject in which students need to concentrate. Below are two games I have allowed my students to play, in order to improve their concentration skills.

Game One: Little Jack Horner

- Ask your students to form a circle, then ask them to sit down.
- You say, 'Little Jack Horner' then clap your hands.
- Once **all** your students have followed your actions and spoken the words, ask the student on your right to repeat the words 'Little Jack Horner' and then click his/her fingers. At the same time, ask the student sitting on your left to say, 'Sat in a corner' and tap his/her head.

The students need to keep their eye on both the left and the right of the circle in order to say the right lines and do the right actions at the right time!

Game Two: Telling Tales

- Your students need to form pairs.
- Both students need to quickly think of a story to tell each other. Perhaps it is something that has happened to them – or the plot of a film they have recently seen, or a book they have read.
- Both students need to tell their tale at the same time, looking each other in the eye.
- If one student looks away, or laughs or hesitates for too long, · then the other is the winner!

There are a number of concentration games that can be played – but just try these before moving on to another activity.

Acting an earlier part of a character's life.

This is useful for students to understand the themes of a play. They might want to think about an event or a theme from 'An Inspector Calls'. Why does Eric take to drink? Your students might like to explore this question by improvising a scene in Eric's earlier childhood where he feels he cannot tell his dad his school problems, because Mr Arthur Birling will not listen.

You could use ideas from books. If you liaise with the English department you might discover that students have studied 'Lord of the Flies'. Perhaps they want to explore what other students at Piggy's school, before the war, thought of him. Your students could improvise a scene at Piggy's school when Piggy was given his nickname.

Kangaroo court

A Kangaroo court is a sham court where an outcome has been determined before the trial. In drama, students can set up a court scene, knowing the outcome of the play. For example, in the play, 'Hamlet', Hamlet's uncle could come to trial for the fact that he murdered the king, Hamlet's father.

Although students know the outcome, the fact that they have set up a judge, jury, prosecutor and defender means that they look at the play from a different angle. They get to know the play better – which is a good revision exercise.

Try Kangaroo court with your students, using the play that they have studied with you.

Drama games

There are many drama games you can allow your students to play. Most of the basic rules of drama room discipline apply. I have mentioned drama room discipline on page 9 and it is worth reminding your students of these before they engage with the games.

Here are some games you can try with your students;

1) *Sounds* (Year 7)

Ask your students to form a circle. Ask them to imagine they are in their bedroom at night, listening to the sounds outside. Can they hear the wind whistling outside? Can they hear the tree branches banging against their window pane? They might hear a train in the distance or a car stopping at traffic lights? They might hear the sound of rain or the beat of music playing in a distant bedroom. Perhaps there is a clock ticking in their room? Ask them to imagine these sounds and to come up with other sounds they might hear from their bedroom.

Now ask them to create a sound with their hands. Give students a few moments to do this and then allow the students who have created the most interesting sounds to demonstrate to the rest of the group.

Now ask them to create a sound with their feet. Again, give them a few minutes to do this and then allow the students who have created the most interesting sounds to demonstrate to the rest of the group.

Finally, ask them to create the sound of wind and rain with their tongues.

When you have given your students a full opportunity to explore sound, ask them to try and create a silence. Ask them what they can hear outside the drama room. After they have told you all they can hear, ask them to experiment with noise. Who can meow like a cat? Bark like a dog? Bray like a donkey?

In pairs, ask your students to take it in turns to create the animal noises. Finally, ask them to demonstrate the noises made.

This exercise should aid concentration. As an additional exercise on sound, ask your students to think of a situation where they might have to communicate without using sound – such as if A has an important message to give to B – but B is waving farewell on a ship that has left port. Your students can experiment using signs and gestures. Perhaps the message could be, 'You have forgotten your passport!'

Now your students can imagine they are in a busy market place. They should be in groups of about four or five. One of them can be the barker – shouting out all he/she is selling, for example, 'bananas only 50p a bunch! Ripe and ready to eat'. Two of the group can be barkers, using as much persuasive language as they can to attract customers. After about three minutes, ask two groups to amalgamate – so there are four barkers and four to six buyers in each group. The object of the game is to see which barker attracts the most customers.

2) *Without words* (Year 7)

Ask your students to work in pairs. They have lost their powers of speech. They are eating a meal at a restaurant. How do they feel about the drinks, the starter, the main meal and the dessert? They can use facial expressions, body language – even grunts and groans.

After a few minutes, ask the pair to stop the improvisation and discuss how effective they were in communicating their thoughts and feelings without language.

As a game (competition) ask them to think of another scenario where they might be able to communicate without language. Showing somebody how to drive, perhaps? The pairs can act out their scenarios and the pair adjudged to be the best could receive a small prize from you!

Explain to your students that they might be on stage miming actions during the course of a play.

3) *The guide* (Year 7)

This is a trust game! Working in pairs, A closes his/her eyes and B guides A around the room – giving whispered instructions to A. B has to make sure A does not bump into anyone or anything. After a few minutes, A and B can swap roles.

4) *What's it like?* (Years 7 and 8)

Students are to show how they feel in a given situation. For example;

What's it like to be too hot?

What's it like to be frozen by the cold north wind?

What's it like to eat something you really dislike?

What's it like to carry something that's too heavy?

As you shout out the sentence, your students should mime what they feel like. This exercise is good for getting students used to being a character in a particular situation.

5) *Making a character*

Choose a line from a play or say something like:

I'm not going to ever do that . . . you shouldn't have asked me!

Tell your students to get into groups of four or five. They can throw in ideas as to why the character has said that sentence and what the character might be like. Perhaps the character is high principled and won't do anything illegal. Or the character might be strong willed and refuses to obey teachers and parents.

Your students must decide, from the one line, what their character is going to be like – how that character might act and behave.

Now throw in another line for a second character –

I've so many regrets – if only I could start all over again!

Your students might conclude that this second character is old and has done regrettable things in the past. Or the character is talking about one event and wants to go back to that one particular morning. Or the character has scored two own goals so the team loses the match!

Once your students have formed their two characters, they can improvise a scene – bringing in two extra characters of their own.

As a game, the group can watch each improvisation and characters can be awarded points out of ten and the improvisation can be awarded points out of ten. Students can use the chart below.

Voice projection				
Gestures				
Pace				
Movement				

Below is an example of a completed chart.

	Old man	Sylvia	Teacher	Policeman
Voice projection	10	8	1	8
Gestures	6	8	6	6
Pace	6	5	4	8
Movement	8	3	1	9

Here is an improvisation chart your students could use.

Quality of play	Interest	Interaction of characters	Use of props	Use of sound/ music

Below is a completed chart.

Quality of play	Interest	Interaction of characters	Use of props	Use of sound/ music
8	8	6	3	0

From the example, your students should deduce that the quality and interest of the play/improvisation was good and the interaction of the characters involved was above average but props were not used to their full advantage and sound/music to evoke mood and atmosphere was non-existent. The above chart would work for up to four groups.

6) *The ship*
This is essentially a concentration game that is full of action and can be quite noisy, as students need to run. If possible, ask them to wear appropriate footwear for this game.

Read out the four parts of a ship and point out that the four corners of the room represent the *starboard*, the *forward*, the *aft* and the *port*. Explain that when you shout 'starboard' your students must run there as fast as possible. The last to reach the right destination is out.

After a few rounds, rapidly shout out positions, to see how many students can avoid becoming confused! For example, shout aft, forward, aft, port, aft, port, starboard!

This exercise will aid listening and concentration skills.

As a variation, tell students that when you shout 'aft' they must always run to port! But when you shout 'port' they must run to 'aft'. However, the other two positions remain the same. See how many are confused!

The crime game

Ask your students to get into groups of four or five. **You** are a television reporter and you are about to give your students an idea of a crime that has occurred. Their task is to re-enact what has taken place. The group judged, by the other groups, to have been the most innovative and imaginative have won!

You say the following:

> The events at 'Sleepy Meadows' are bizarre in the extreme. Locals were shocked when they woke up this morning to discover that a hideous crime took place in their small village. There is a dead man, an unused and new gibbet fixed up outside their local store and a car without an engine or wheels upside down on their village green. In the duck pond, police discovered a sword, an empty jewel box, a dark cloak and a lantern. Why and how this man was murdered, we have no clue . . . except that . . .

Tell your students that, at this point there is a power cut and they need to reconstruct the crime using **all** the clues given. When I have done this exercise with my students I have found they can be very inventive. For example, the man was a rich aristocrat who boasted about his jewels and his wealth. He was murdered, the jewels were taken and the murdered man was bundled into the car – but the thieves crashed the car, and in a panic threw the man out of the car and dumped the empty jewel box in the duck pond. They then fled. Meanwhile, car thieves stole the engine and wheels. They were intercepted by a local, whom they threatened to hang and made up a temporary gibbet. They still hold him hostage in the local park! See if your students come up with a better scenario!

Stealing the ball

Ask your group to sit in a circle. A student is chosen to shut his/her eyes (or preferably, is blindfolded). That student sits in the middle of the circle. A second student is chosen. This student has to creep up and attempt to steal the ball. That student then needs to go around the outer edge of the circle and get back to his/her place without the blindfolded student hearing a sound. Should the first student hear a sound and point at the second student, that student is out.

After a few rounds, you can speed the game up by having two thieves attempting to steal the ball. For a competitive element, the blindfolded student that notices the most thieves is the winner. A blindfolded student is only out when the thief steals the ball and returns to his/her place.

This game does aid concentration. You do need space for a wide circle, so that 'clever' thieves do not simply stretch out for the ball!

Time

We all need time to think. Ideas do not always come quickly. My observation of drama lessons has been that sometimes drama teachers expect students to come up with excellent ideas within a few minutes. Sometimes it is useful for students to have a pen and paper handy, to write down 'thought-showers'. They can do this individually or in small groups. At other times, it is good to give them some structured or unstructured ideas. Ideas do not always need to be verbal. For instance, a piece of classical music might stimulate the students to think of ideas that the music might suggest. I have discovered that pictures or photographs can suggest ideas and stimulate thought. A picture of an activity, such as cavemen hunting, or the photograph of a busy market scene, or a famous painting (perhaps a Pre-Raphaelite) – or the photograph of an older person holding a baby might allow the students' imaginations to soar!

Another method I have used is to select newspaper headlines such as (for example);

- 'Headless Cat Stalks Mouse' or
- 'Boy Saved From Drowning By Dog' or
- 'New Earth-like Planet Discovered.'

Even when you have given the general outline for a piece of work, students still need that valuable thinking time!

Students working together

When working together, allow students to think further than the script or the improvisation. Get them thinking about using practical techniques to improve their work. These are as follows;

1) *Sequencing*

When working without scripts, there is going to be a problem in that the students might all want to speak at once, or not know when to come in! They need to talk through their ideas and check that there is an established order of events. The storyline they have chosen needs to be presented in a logical sequence.

When working with younger students, you might need to ask them to decide in what order each one will be speaking.

2) *The dramatic pause*

When speaking, a short pause can be created for effect. It can help to build up tension. Students need to be reminded that silences can be just as effective as words spoken. However, too many dramatic pauses can lose their effect and become tedious.

Examples of the use of a dramatic pause can be;

- I know who murdered Damien Lorne – (*dramatic pause*) – it was his own brother!

And;

- After many years of wandering through the jungle of life, I returned home to my village – (*dramatic pause*) – only to discover that my village was in ruins and my friends all gone!

Initially, students need to build in a dramatic pause. There can be a tendency for a student to not realize that another student is using one and to cover the silence with their own words. This interruption can ruin an intended dramatic effect and the tension is lost. To avoid this, students can mention to the group that they intend to use a dramatic pause.

Ask your students to work in groups and improvise a scene, using the dramatic pause once or twice, for moments of tension in their story. A scene might be one of the following;

- Damien Lorne's body has been discovered and the suspects are gathered in one room. A clever detective is sifting through the evidence.
- A villager is telling others about his life after he left the village.
- Two teenagers have discovered an alien spacecraft and two aliens are about to emerge from the craft.

Blocking in

In small groups, your students can work to decide where they will stand during their chosen improvisation. They need to place themselves where they can be seen and heard.

Your students might consider symbolic blocking in. A boss of a large company might be placed on a higher level than his employees. A King and Queen might be placed centre stage, with courtiers placed downstage. For example;

Guards	King and Queen	Guards
	Courtiers	
Servants		Servants

Thinking about blocking in ensures that your students do not stand in a huddle, bunched together, during a performance.

Facing out of the drama

For prepared improvisations, your students can work out when members of the group can face out of the drama. All this means is that the students who are not involved with the immediate action of the drama, can stand out and face upstage. Effectively, their backs are to the audience – so it is obvious to the audience that they are not involved in the action at that particular moment. It cuts down the use of entrances and exits and it will make the action less disjointed. When those 'facing out' turn and speak, this can be quite effective, too.

Your students can decide how to gain the maximum impact by using this technique when working through their ideas.

Noise collage

In this technique, different sounds can be created by other actors that overlap the actor's voices. This idea can create a dramatic effect if used only once or twice – during an important moment in the play or during the improvisation. For example, if a girl is talking to her mother about the fact that she might be pregnant, other actors can create sounds associated with pregnancy or children. The sounds might be thoughts that float into the girl's head when she is talking. Or thoughts might be whispered by the actors to suggest the thoughts that whirl around the girl's head – such as;

> 'Dad will kill me,' and 'How can I do well at school now?' or , 'How do I look after a baby?'

A group I taught several years ago took as their theme a car accident in which a passenger died. They combined the sounds and whispering voices to great effect.

Tip: The sounds and whispered words must never drown out the words spoken by the students in the action. In the example of the girl talking to her mother, the lines spoken by both the girl and the mother must be clearly heard. Sounds and whispers are most effective when they are in the background.

Ask your students to use this technique in a scene concerning a teacher talking to a student about lack of homework.

Working through ideas – practical

Ask your students to split into groups of four or five. Tell them that they are going to work on ideas concerning a haunted house. Allow them both individual and group thinking time, then ask the group to jot down ideas and work out who says what and when. They also need to decide where on stage the lines will be delivered.

In the improvisation, they should include –

- Sequencing
- The dramatic pause
- Blocking in
- Facing out
- A noise collage

Ask each group to act out their improvisation and the watching group can mark their performance using the chart below;

	Student 1	Student 2	Student 3	Student 4	Student 5
Voice projection					
Dramatic pause					
Blocking in					
Facing out					
Noise collage					
Overall quality of the performance					

Each student can be given a mark out of ten by each group. Student 1 (for example), can be replaced by the student name or the name given to the student in the role play.

Working in groups
Teacher management
I usually ask students to work in groups of four or five, so that there are enough students to plan and take on character roles for both improvisation (planned and unplanned) and for scripted work. Sometimes students need to take on more than one role. Occasionally, if there are uneven numbers of students, I will allow a group of six. For example, at Key Stage Three, there might be a drama class of thirty. That would make six groups of five – which is manageable. If there are thirty-one students in a class, this would make five groups of five and one of six! For thirty-two students in a class, you might want four groups of five and two groups of six or eight groups of four. Personally, I found eight groups of four unmanageable if there is only one adult in the room. However, this can depend upon the activity!

I have allowed friendship groups to work together but, with mixed ability classes, I have sometimes spread the talent. Occasionally, students fall out and refuse to work with each other. If students cannot resolve their differences quickly and between themselves, in a civilized manner, I have given them time out of drama and presented them with a written task. Usually (to my amazement at times) the problems have been resolved and they have been more than ready to rejoin their group.

During my drama lessons, I give students the illusion that they are working professionals and need to cooperate together. The students are instructed to work with everyone in the class. There are no exceptions! The penalty of refusing to work in a group or with an individual is to sit out the drama, work on a written task and face further appropriate action – such as a letter home, a detention or a session with the head of year. The action depends upon the severity of the case and school policy.

Student management

I make it clear to students that they need to engage with the subject matter. When I first meet a new group, I tend to give them short scripts to work with and ask them to work on **planned** improvisations with a step by step guide. They need to work together and fill in the details – for example;

The Bully
- Scene One – the bully comes from a home with a violent father.
- Scene Two shows us that the bully has no real friends – he's mostly avoided.
- Scene Three – the bully picks on 'weaker' students, who are all afraid of him.
- Scene Four shows us that the bully makes weaker students steal for him.
- Scene Five – a new student arrives at the school. He is immediately popular, being good at sport and in his lessons. He is also kind and generous. He is what the bully might have been like in a parallel universe!
- Scene Six – the bully attempts to dominate the newcomer, who stands up for himself.
- Scene Seven – the bully's ways (both bullying and enticing others to steal) are discovered and he is in trouble. He is suitably punished.
- Scene Eight – the bully's father is jailed for a serious criminal offence. There is a chance for the bully to have a new start in life.

With a simple plan, such as the one above, students are able to use their imaginations to fill in the details. However, if you want them to work with prepared scripts that allow them to work on dramatic techniques, the books I have used are – 'Page to Stage' and 'Scripts and Sketches'.

Reading and acting out full scripts

When working on full scripts, your students need to read through the scripts a few times and, if possible, highlight their part in the play. Below is a method I have used with my students;

- First reading of a script by student volunteers.
- A talk about the script, its themes and issues and the language used in the play.

- Allocation of parts and jobs.
- Questions – to check understanding.
- Either watching a version of the play from a televised production or a film – or going to a theatre to see a production of the play. (To be honest – this stage is not always possible!)
- Second reading of the script – students have the opportunity to ask questions about the script and/or the language used.
- Taking some scenes and looking at them in close detail. Discussing what dramatic techniques could be used to enhance the performance. For example, in which scenes could we use 'Facing Out'? Would 'Facing Out' be desirable in this particular play? Where could we *naturally* use a dramatic pause? Would a noise collage be appropriate in any scene?

This process allows the students to interpret the play in their own way.

- Students may wish to take notes, or make notes on the script at this point.
- For school production, I have drawn up a rehearsal schedule so that students have a good knowledge of where they need to be on stage at a particular time. I can also check that lines are being learned!
- Students will need a full rehearsal, a lighting, music and costume rehearsal.
- Just before a play is shown to a live audience, a full dress rehearsal is in order!
- Finally, the play is performed.

For an examination piece, some of the above stages can be combined.

A play in a day

I was once involved in a play in a day. I had to act out a small part, learn my lines and know where to be on stage all in a school day! At the end of the day, I had to perform in front of a group of drama students – who could judge the performance of each actor. The script was 'Punch and Judy' and the first I knew about it was when, as a drama teacher, I turned up for a drama INSET! The experience was both exhilarating and scary.

Since that day, I have used this idea with my students using a variety of scripts. I urge you to try this out! You will need to plan well ahead. Start by asking the Senior Management Team to allow you and your students a day away from the prescribed curriculum in order to do this! Show them the attainment targets they will hit when doing this task. If a school has activities week at the end of the summer term, you may be able to use one of those days with some students opting to do a play in a day. Or you could encourage your Year 10 drama group to do this!

In my experience, you need to be the director. In my opinion, the *Punch and Judy* Script is a good one to use. If you use an old original script, there should be no copyright problems. The Punch and Judy Script can be found on the companion website. It first appeared in London Labour and the London Poor and was published by Henry Mayhew in 1851. I have adapted the script to suit our purposes. It is difficult, as the dialect words are a problem for some students to reproduce and with some groups, you might need to rework parts of the dialect. I have actually kept dialect in. I suggest you go through the words in a first reading of the script.

Also, although Punch and Judy shows still go on, some of the concepts might appear a little un-P.C. these days. Again, I tell students that humour has changed over the years and a humorous view of wife-beating, baby-bashing and violence was seen in the context of slap-stick humour. Please note that strong dialect has altered the spelling!

Your students will need to appoint somebody to be in charge of sound effects, lighting, props, costumes, make-up and sets. They will certainly need a stage manager – who should be reliable and calm. Each student should be allocated a job. Perhaps some students will need to assist others, such as an assistant stage manager.

Ask your students to read through the script, then put into practice all that they've learned. They need to ask themselves the following;

- What sound effects are needed and how are these effects going to be achieved?
- What lighting is needed? How are we going to get the right lighting for the various scenes? How can we keep it simple?
- What props are needed? Is it a good idea to use props chairs for the individual actors and for the person we appoint stage manager?
- Can we find and use costumes?
- Can we use make-up?
- Can we construct simple sets? What type of set(s) would be best for this play?
- Are we able to make use out of dramatic techniques, such as the dramatic pause, blocking in, facing out of the drama and a noise collage?

The students need to be realistic in that the play has to be read, understood and performed in one day.

Eight students from the class need to be picked to act out the play and (if possible) learn their lines for the performance. They may need to adlib rather than learn the script word perfectly. Or they may decide to act out the play using their scripts.

A reminder: Your students will need to appoint somebody to be in charge of sound effects, lighting, props, costumes, make-up and sets. They will also need a stage manager. There should be no one without a job. For instance, the student in charge of make-up will need plenty of helpers.

For a Year 10 or 11 group, this task will certainly be demanding and will require complete concentration and focus on the task in hand. The students will need to learn fast –they will have to put into practice all the techniques they have mastered so far! Your Year 12 and 13 groups will find this task demanding, too! The end product does not need to be a polished performance (how can it be?) but the object of the exercise is really the process of learning.

A thought: If you wish to work longer (more than just one day) on the script, your students could make or borrow masks or puppets and give a traditional performance – to show to younger students.

Working in groups

Apart from delivering monologues and solo-performances, drama is all about group work. Ideally, all students should work together. When I have had a new group for drama, I get them used to the idea of working together as quickly as I possibly can. If they refuse, then I go through the discipline route that I have indicated earlier. I initially encourage different groups to work together. For example, I ask all those who have a birthday in March to raise their hands – then say, 'right, you are a group'. I can pre-arrange groups, using the register to have birthday groups working together or check on student ability and have them working on a mixed ability basis. I allow friendship groups too. It really depends upon the group and the task that I have in mind.

Some of my early work with a new Key Stage Three group would be circle work. However, improvisations work well with groups of about four or five.

Should you find your drama group difficult, place them into groups and spread out the difficult members of the group. Then give them some ideas and ask them to come up with an improvised piece, using the dramatic techniques outlined in this book, within a certain time limit. If they fail to achieve work matching up to your required standards, have them rehearse the piece in their own time, to be ready for the next drama lesson. Make sure though, that you outline your standards beforehand!

You could print out a sheet of standards for group work.

- You must enter the room in an orderly manner and form a circle, sitting on the floor.
- Stop when I give the signal.
- Be prepared to share ideas.
- Be prepared to work with everyone and anyone within the class.
- Know that groups are not 'fixed'.
- Be prepared to evaluate each group and each individual performance.
- Know that you have to work to a time limit.

Please do adapt according to your students' needs and your own needs. I found that the above set of standards worked for me!

Try your group on the following ideas for improvisation and problem-solving work.

Improvisation

1) An elf from an enchanted forest meets an evil Ork and an explorer. They need to steal the dragon's gold.
2) Re-read 'Young Again' (page 27) and work out the second scene – it will include Oswald, the elf, the King and his daughter.

Problem solving

1) Mrs Myles does not want her daughter (son) to attend a party. All her (his) friends are going. What should he (she) do? Improvise and act out the scene.
2) There are three tickets for a sporting fixture at Wembley. Five friends wish to go. How can this problem be resolved? Improvise a scene where tough decisions are made.

Tell your students they have exactly half an hour to work out whichever idea they are using. After that time, they need to act out the chosen scene to your satisfaction, using appropriate dramatic techniques.

CHAPTER 7

Engaging the students

Word games

I have always recognized that students enjoy word games. Here are two they might like to try.

1) *The alliteration game*

Ask your students to form a circle. One student stands in the middle of the circle, you choose a letter from the alphabet. Time your student two minutes – during that two minutes, your student needs to name as many words beginning with the chosen letter. No repeats are allowed. The student who wins is the one who has thought of as many words as possible in the time allowed. For example – E.

Egg, edge, Easter, east, eaves and so on.

Tip: Borrow a stop-watch and ask a student to be the timer.

2) *Playing the alphabet*

Keep your students in the circle and ask one student to stand in the middle of the circle. Choose a letter of the alphabet. The player in the centre must come up with the name of a person then an object that can be sold in a particular place.

For example, B.

Briony (person) sells biscuits (object) in Bulgaria (place).

Counting games

Students generally enjoy counting games. Here are two I have used with my students – and are their favourites.

1) *Count to twenty*

Students form a circle. They need to face outwards, so they cannot see each other. The group then need to count to twenty – one student saying one number at a time.

Select a student to start the count, another random student says the following number and so on. If more than one person speaks at the same time, the group need to start again at number one.

Tip: If you feel the students are cheating, ask them to close their eyes!

For a variation (and a more difficult task) ask your students to count backwards from twenty!

2) *Object making*

Call out the name of an object and ask the group to quickly form the shape of that object while you slowly count from 1–10. All the group need to be involved in making that shape. The shapes I have found the students enjoy making are;

- An octopus
- An aeroplane
- A peacock
- A butterfly
- A firework

After a few rounds, ask your students what shape they'd like to make. They do come up with some interesting ideas!

This game aids group co-operation and concentration. Students are focused; working together and thinking quickly.

Storytelling

Storytelling is part of drama and students usually enjoy this activity. I often start groups off by asking them to sit in a circle and I then give them a sentence, such as 'Green faced aliens landed yesterday.' I will then ask another student to continue until everyone in the circle has completed a sentence. I then tell them that they have created a story.

Still in their circle, I ask students to tell me a story that they know – either from a real event or from a book they have read or from a film they have seen.

Having heard the stories, I then go through storytelling techniques. These are as follows;

- Look around your audience and give them a welcoming smile!
- Create an atmosphere as soon as possible by using music or by darkening the room.

- When you begin, allow your eyes to move slowly over your audience. Keep eye contact all the time.
- Set the scene for your audience by starting with a time and place.
- Begin in a dramatic way. As you tell your story, keep it interesting, so the audience will continue to wonder what will happen next.
- Tell your story as if it actually happened to you – or to somebody you know really well.
- Your voice is really important – make sure you change its pace and volume. At times, make it melodic and interesting.
- Use facial expressions to show the feelings of your characters and their natures and personalities. Show, through your facial expressions, the situations your characters find themselves in.
- If characters speak, use interesting 'character' voices. Try to engage the audience so that they feel sympathy or hatred for the characters involved in the story.
- Use sounds: for instance rub your hands together to create the sound of rain.
- Use emotional sounds: such as sobs, sighs and yawns.
- Use the pregnant pause between words – to create a dramatic effect.
- Make sure you look at the audience and around the audience – with expectation. Surprise them once or twice by making a loud noise – or speak in whispers occasionally.
- Involve your audience with phrases such as, 'As you know . . . forests are dark deep and dangerous'.

Ask your students to get into groups of four or five and try the following;

The old man sat alone at the edge of the forest, shivering in the half-dark. The stars shone and the frost fell like gossamer. He could hear voices . . . but they were not the harsh voices of the workhouse, they were voices from the past.

He reflected on the ship that took him to the fitful head, where the old woman told him to look through the sleet and the frost and make his fortune in Greenland. And when he'd sailed, what then? The ship hit a rock and sank like a stone. The crew drowned but he'd swum for his life. So much for the old woman and her ability to tell the future.

He swam to an island. He reached the sandy shore and flopped down like a flounder – exhausted, spent. There, on the heather clad headland was a man digging for peat. He called and the man came to him, giving him warmth and shelter. There he joined the fishing fleets and returned to his native Yorkshire.

Time passsed, and his wandering spirit made him sign up for the whaling ships. Before long, he sailed south to pick up a new crew at Margate. There, he met his bride and left the ships for good.

But what cruelty was time? Now an old man, he'd wandered from the Thanet workhouse to spy on life for one last time. One last time – before they'd take him back, to work out the last of his days – in these dark Victorian times, where the rich get richer and the poor are forgotten.

Ask your students to split into pairs and read the piece above. They need to look again at the bullet points for storytelling delivery techniques. Can they change the script to ask questions? Or engage the audience, such as, 'As you know, in those dark Victorian times . . .'

Now ask them to read the story, 'The Twelve Brothers' which is available on the companion website. In groups of about four or five, they need to decide how the story can be told using every member of their group. They must decide if they will have one narrator and engage the rest of the group by having them mime the action or perhaps they could spit the story into parts, so that all of them will have a go at reading it. Or perhaps the story can be told partly by using a chorus. They could incorporate a few of the above ideas or think of different ways to present the story.

The groups should watch each other perform and use the chart below to judge their performances. They can give a mark out of ten.

Title: *The Twelve Brothers*

	Student 1	Student 2	Student 3	Student 4
Use of facial expression				
Use of voice –variety and character				
Use of hand/body gestures				
Creating an atmosphere				
Use of sound/music				

As an additional activity, your students might like to work in groups and re-write the story as a short play. Below is a possible start:

The Twelve Brothers

(*Scene One, the Royal Palace, throne room*)

King: (*to his wife*) We have had twelve sons and all I want is a daughter! I want to spoil a royal princess.

Queen: (*pats her stomach*) Perhaps, this time, we shall have a little princess.

King: (*enthusiastic*) We shall have a girl – lucky thirteen! If this child is a girl, we'll kill all our sons!

Queen: (*shocked*) No! Why, my husband and wise king, would you want to murder our children?

King: I do not want our kingdom divided into thirteen when we die. If all our lands are divided amongst thirteen children – then there wouldn't be much for anyone. The kingdom would be weak, ripe for invasion. Our enemies would be laughing!

Queen: (*upset*) But I love our sons!

King: (*determined*) They shall *all* die. I have decided. The unborn princess will have great possessions and great power. She shall rule this land as a strong queen after my death. I'll call for a carpenter.

Queen: (*confused*) A carpenter?

King: We shall have twelve coffins made, so that we shall be prepared if the unborn child is a girl.

Queen: (*very upset*) This is so horrible!

(*The Queen runs from the royal throne room in tears. She almost collides into her youngest son, Benjamin.*)

Benjamin: (*thinking*) I wonder what's bothering mum!

Ask your students to continue writing the script. When completed, they can act it out and judge each group's performance.

Tongue twisters

Your students will love trying tongue twisters! They are fun to try and help younger students to speak clearly. Tell them, it isn't the speed the tongue twisters are spoken – the trick is to speak them clearly.

Working in pairs, ask your students to try out the following tongue twisters – some of them are well known.

- The Leith police dismisseth us.
- Rubber baby-buggy bouncers.
- I saw Susie sitting in a shoe shine shop. Where she sits she shines, and where she shines she sits.
- The skunk sat on the stump. The stump thunk the skunk stunk. The skunk thunk the stump stunk. What stunk – the skunk or the stump?

- The sixth Sheik's sixth sheep's sick.
- How can a cram cram in a clean cream can?
- Denise sees the fleece, Denise sees the fleas. At least Denise could sneeze and feed and freeze the fleas.
- How much wood could a woodchuck chuck, if a woodchuck could chuck wood?
- Can you can a can as a canner can can a can?
- Roberta ran rings around the roman ruins.
- Peter Piper picked a peck of pickled peppers. If Peter Piper picked a peck of pickled peppers, where's the peck of pickled peppers Peter Piper picked?

Further games: *forming groups*

Play music and when the music stops, ask the class to form into groups by shouting out a number. You might shout out 'six' and the class needs to form into a group of six. Those who fail are out. You then ask the six to do something – such as sing a song or hop around the room on one leg, or form a circle. Before you shout out the next number, those who are out are back in the game! When you want the game to end, shout out a number you wish them to be in for another activity. In this way, you can divide your students into working groups – it will avoid moans, as they have chosen the group themselves!

Calling

Ask your class to divide equally into groups. Give them a few moments to work out a secret call sign they will all recognize. It could be an owl hoot or a dog bark. Then ask them all to come to the centre of the room. Allow them to walk around the room (perhaps doing a silly walk) then shout 'Lie down'. Tell your students to close their eyes. They then have to call each other. They need to crawl towards each other and get into their original group, without opening their eyes. The first group to have attracted all the members together wins!

What is the object?

Prepare a tray with about fifteen different objects on the tray. The objects could be a tube of toothpaste, an orange, a slab of toffee, a shoe . . . and so on. Keep the tray in your cupboard, or out of the way! Ask your class to divide into about four equal groups. They need to close their eyes! Then bring on the tray, asking one member from each group to select one object, feel the object and try to guess what it is. The group that guesses the most objects wins!

Thought tracking

Your students will discover that thought tracking is useful in that it allows them to think aloud – helping them to understand their character. They can explore their characters' motivations. They are also able to explore their characters' feelings about the situation they find themselves in; as well as the hopes of their characters, the issues and fears of those characters at a particular moment.

You may ask a group to freeze the action and get them to explore their characters' attitudes and motivations at a particular moment – or they may wish to freeze a moment themselves.

Thought tracking encourages students to know their character well, rather than just saying the lines. This means that when they do speak the lines, their delivery will have **impact** because they will understand **how** the lines need to be delivered. This encourages students to develop the characters they are portraying.

Your students can explore their characters' **inner** thoughts. By speaking out their perceived inner thoughts, students are better placed to understand their characters. This process also allows other actors in the scene to understand the other characters in the play much better. Thought tracking can be used in both scripted and unscripted pieces.

When Lady Macbeth speaks her soliloquy ('Macbeth', Act One, Scene V) she is actually speaking her inner thoughts and conveying what she is thinking to the audience – so that they understand her reasoning and her motivation for persuading her husband to kill King Duncan. She is almost thought tracking!

Lady Macbeth is reading and reflecting on a letter, sent to her from Macbeth. He is telling her that after a great battle, he met three witches who told him that he would become king in the near future.

Lady Macbeth: Glamis thou art, and Cawdor; and shalt be what thou art
    promis'd.
Yet do I fear thy nature;
It is too full o'th' milk of human kindness
To catch the nearest way. Thou wouldst
be great;
Art not without ambition, but without
The illness should attend it.

In those lines, Lady Macbeth is saying that Macbeth has been given two titles the witches said he would have but that he is too kind to kill the king (catch the nearest way). She knows he is ambitious but not to the extent that he would kill the king and claim the crown. She is speaking her inner-most thoughts here! She goes on to say;

That I may pour my spirits in thine ear,
And chastise with the valour of my tongue
All that impedes thee from the golden round

She tells the audience that she intends to fill him with her evil thoughts and nag him until he gains the crown (the golden round) by murdering the king!

Ask your students to work in groups of four or five and act out the scene from '*The Big Match*'. They should freeze the action at any point in the short extract and thought track each character. Then they can freeze the action at the end of the play and re-thought track the action.

Granddad: I used to enjoy a football match.

Dad: So did I. Times have changed. Some of today's yobs are only good for a punch up.

Ken: That's not fair. I'll bet there was trouble in your day.

Dad: Not to the same extent. We could walk to a match in peace. We could travel by train and just talk about our team. We became excited and boisterous, but we didn't use violence. Today's youths don't want to watch a decent game. They just go to a match to cause trouble.

Jill: But dad, Ken and I *are* today's youth. We're not out for violence.

Dad: Yes, but you've been brought up well. Some of today's youngsters have more money than sense.

Ken: But dad, if we went – you and I – we'd keep out of trouble.

Dad: You can't help becoming involved, son. Once a crowd of hooligans pick on you, there isn't much you can do about it.

Ken: I won't wear my supporter's scarf. Nobody would know what side I was on.

Dad: No, we're not going to a match and my decision is final.

Granddad: Cup final? That's not 'til May!

Jill: He said 'that's final' granddad. He won't go to a real match with Ken.

Granddad: Albert always was mean. I'll pay for the lad to go with his mates.

Ken: A great idea – hey, dad?

Mum: You don't understand, granddad. A football match is just an excuse for a punch up these days.

Dad: Exactly! Much better to watch the match on TV.

Granddad: The lad has to learn. Why, during the war . . . !

Dad: You keep out of it! No lad of mine is risking life and limb at a football match. Much better to keep well away from trouble.

Ken: It just isn't fair.

Now ask your students to think about how each character might act in the following scenario;

Three miners are trapped 2,000 feet below the earth's surface. It is late August, they are unlikely to be rescued for at least a month. One is an older miner. He was due for retirement. His brother is seriously ill and not likely to survive. The old miner had hoped to see him for one last time. Another miner's wife is due to give birth any day now. He'd hoped to see the birth of his baby. The youngest miner is afraid they'll all die.

Ask your students to improvise a scene as the three discuss the situation they are in. Your students can thought track at any point.

Thought tunnel

Creating a thought tunnel allows the students to think about a particular character in a play. Thought tunnels can be used for improvised pieces and for scripted work. Students can create a tunnel by forming two parallel lines and touching finger tips with the person opposite. A student takes on a character and the group whispers what that character might be thinking in a scene from the play. Take Ken, from 'The Big Match'. As he walks slowly through the tunnel, each member of the tunnel needs to say something.

- It's not fair. I wanna see a live football match.
- Granddad knows how I feel.
- I'm going to let my mates down!
- My mates will think I'm a baby.
- Dad's a coward, he's scared, that's why he won't take me.
- It was nice of granddad to pay for me and my mates.

Or students can thought tunnel a play as a whole – useful for revision. They can thought tunnel Lady Macbeth.

- I'll have to nag my husband before he'll kill the king.
- I'd like to be Queen!
- Evil has entered me . . . now I can be cruel.
- Why didn't Macbeth involve me in Banquo's murder?
- He doesn't love me anymore!
- There is nothing left to live for.

By thought tunnelling, students can learn from each other. Also they (or you) can pick up, by what is said, if a particular student has misunderstood aspects of a play.

Soliloquies and monologues

A soliloquy is a speech delivered by a character in a play while alone. Sometimes, a soliloquy is used by a character who is talking to him/herself and disregarding (or oblivious of) any listeners. Shakespeare used the soliloquy when characters were on stage alone. He used it as a device to show the audience the inner-most thoughts of a character. A famous example is from the play 'Hamlet'. Hamlet is talking about the possibility of suicide because he is devastated by his father's death. He goes on to compare the new king, his uncle, with his father, the dead king. Hamlet's mother has married Claudius, the new king of Denmark, very shortly after her husband's death.

Ask your students to read Hamlet's soliloquy and then ask them to take turns to deliver the soliloquy. This work is suitable for an A or A/S level drama group.

Hamlet: O, that this too too solid flesh would melt,
Thaw, and resolve itself into a dew!
Or that the Everlasting had not fix'd
His canon 'gainst self-slaughter! O God! God!
How weary, stale, flat, and unprofitable,
Seem to me all the uses of this world!
Fie on't! Ah, fie! 'tis an unweeded garden,
That grows to seed; things rank and gross in nature
Possess it merely. That it should come to this!
But two months dead! Nay, not so much, not two.
So excellent a king that was to this
Hyperion to a satyr; so loving to my mother,
That he might not between the winds of heaven
Visit her face too roughly. Heaven and earth!
Must I remember? Why, she would hang on him.
As if of appetite had grown
By what it fed on; and yet, within a month –
Let me not think on't. Frailty, thy name is woman!–
A little month, or ere those shoes were old
With which she followed my poor father's body,
Like Niobe, all tears –why she, even she –
O God! A beast that wants discourse of reason
Would have mourn'd longer – married with my uncle,
My father's brother; but no more like my father
Than I to Hercules. Within a month,
Ere yet the salt of most unrighteous tears
Had left the flushing in her galled eyes,
She married. O, most wicked speed, to post
With such dexterity to incestuous sheets!
It is not, nor it cannot come to good.
But break, my heart, for I must hold my tongue.

Before delivering the soliloquy, if possible, show your students some recent examples of 'Hamlet' particularly this speech, from Act One,

Scene Two. They should look at the variety of intonations and how the actor uses the pregnant pause for effect. For a reminder of how to deliver a speech, students should look back at page 97.

Students can use a thought tunnel here, so that as 'Hamlet' walks through the thought tunnel, other actors can point out what Hamlet is thinking at this point and how he is feeling.

For examples of monologues, your group should look at the following two creative ideas;

The first is an idea that emerged after studying the play, *Cat on a Hot Tin Roof* by Tennessee Williams. Brick was a sporting hero who had taken to drink and a man who'd become disillusioned with life. His father, Big Daddy – once a solid fortress, was dying of cancer – but nobody wanted to confront the truth concerning his illness. Apart from Brick and his mother, the other characters only want Big Daddy's inheritance.

Requiem For Brick

Me, I was dedicated to winning.
My victories were glorious. I never contemplated defeat!
Yet defeat, like a winged phantom,
Silently settled beside me.

She came as I ran into the changing room – sweating and
Palpitating – savouring my last win.
My last hurrah!

Then, on one hot moonlit night,
I hobbled off.
Other players, concerned only for a moment,
Burst back into the game I no longer commanded.

But we were still a team – then – in those days . . .
Until my wife betrayed me.
So, I finally surrendered –
Could no longer deliver.

My pure love destroyed,
My ideal in ruins.
My life shattered,
My firm foundations undermined.

My life shattered
Like an empty bottle, smashed
By some wayside tramp.

Drunk and confused,
I enjoy a kind of solitude,
Waiting for the final click

That will release me from my burden.
Bringing peace.

Should pour myself another drink,
Watch my father die.

He never knew me,
Never could know me.
Even in those days,
When he watched with a father's pride . . .
He never understood
Why I risked all
For a purity
Incomprehensible for one such as he!

I'll pour another drink,
Fill another glass.

Task: Working in groups, allow your students to think about and work out strategies for understanding and delivering this monologue.

The second example is a reflective monologue – an older person looking back at his youth.

Fell Walks Past

I am out there.

We are out there – climbing rocks – feeling the cold air
and raw wind
upon our cheeks.
Sniffing the December air like wild animals,
The cold biting into our bones,
Freezing our thoughts
Like something out of Hell.

Our young unconquered spirits danced
Past trees, rivers, valleys, crags . . .
We sang with the waterfalls and the morning frost
As we raced past hikers, climbers – punishing our bodies
Carefree, existing for the moment.

There is still a wind out there,
Calling me like a siren's song.
Snow capped Pen-y-ghent
And the cold breezes from Whernside
And the rocks of Ingleborough
And the weak winter sunsets
And the pub where we rested
Beside a warm wood and a coal fire.

The image fades as I test my new car
And think of a film we might see
In our heated home.
Or flick through holiday brochures,
ticking off another foreign destination.
Or watch the sunset with fading eyesight
While those cold places are taken by younger walkers.

Ask your students to read '*Fell Walks Past*' through carefully.

How is this monologue meant to be delivered? In small groups, students should take it in turns to read the monologue before delivering it either individually or as a group activity. If your students wish to deliver a monologue as a group activity they might like to ask themselves – do we intend to read it as a chorus or should each of us take on a section? They need to ask themselves which is the best method for audience impact.

For younger students, the monologue below might be more appropriate.

Special Powers
Hi, I'm Sam and everyone has special powers except me.
Mum told me just yesterday that Grandma can talk the hind legs
Off a donkey. Well, I can't do that!

Dad said that he smelt a rat when someone tried to sell him a cheap car.
He's lucky, I can't smell animals. I didn't even see the rat.

Jeff, at school, says he turns green when somebody picks at their scabs.
I can't change colour! I haven't even been around when he has!
So, I'm unlucky too!

Wendy tells me her Uncle Bert just hung-on in there after his heart op.
But I can't act like a bat and I'm not ill like her uncle.

Our Mike was over the moon
When he got promoted at work.
But I can't jump as far as the bedroom ceiling,

Helen said her new boyfriend was out of this world,
But I can't spot aliens – it just isn't fair.

I don't think it's right,
Everyone has special powers . . . except me.

Working in small groups, your students should get the humour of the monologue. Knowing it is humorous, does it need to be delivered in a particular way? Now they should take it in turns to deliver the monologue.

Seven deadly sins

I have discovered that students enjoy scripting plays using the theme of the seven deadly sins.

From the fourteenth century onwards, the seven deadly sins have been acted out and made into plays.

The seven deadly sins are as follows: wrath, greed, sloth, pride, lust, envy and gluttony. Ask your students to work in groups of about four or five and decide upon the definitions of the seven deadly sins. They can use a dictionary if they wish. After they have understood the meaning of the sins, they can take one of the sins and write a short script, using the sin as a theme. Here are two examples;

'*Sloth*' by Janice Oakshore and Alice Gurney

(The class are in their history lesson. Janice is sitting at her desk, daydreaming.)

Alice: (*whispers to Janice*) Shouldn't you be working on the project. It needs to be handed in tomorrow.

Janice: (*shrugs her shoulders*) I haven't even started yet. Can't be bothered.

Alice: (*puzzled*) But you used to work so hard!

Mr Mould: (*stern*) Quiet, Alice Gurney!

Alice: Sorry sir. (*whispers to Janice*) It's ever since you met that Simon De'Ville isn't it?

(*Later, in the school canteen. Janice is speaking to Simon.*)

Simon: (*slurps his coke*) Hey, Janice, let's bunk off school. We could listen to some music round my place. Mum's out at the betting shop.

Janice: (*drinks her coke*) We can't just bunk off school.

Simon: (*laughs*) Why not? Work isn't for everyone.

Janice: We might get caught. Anyway, I ought to do *some* work.

Simon: (*laughs*) Work? Much better to chill, relax and enjoy ourselves. You only live once, eh? I can't be bothered with work!

Janice: (*laughs nervously*) Nor can I!

Simon: Come over to my place then. You haven't seen my place yet. You'll be in for a treat. You know where I live? (*Janice nods*)Number 45. See you in about half an hour.

Janice: (*surprised*) Half an hour? But it's only a five minute walk.

Simon: Yeah, well, a five minute walk takes energy. I'd rather get the bus. Besides, I need to tidy the place up. Mum is so slothful!

(*Half an hour later, Simon and Janice sit in Simon's lounge. Music is playing. She inspects a glass of coke he's given her. It looks dirty and dusty.*)

Janice: (*holding the glass to the light*) The glass looks – kind of – unclean.

Simon: (*laughs*) Oh, all the glasses in this house are dirty. Mum and I don't do washing up.

Janice: (*glances around her*) This place – it's in a bit of a mess.

Simon: (*surprised*) Do you think so? Mum can't be bothered to tidy them up, I suppose.

Janice: The kitchen – to be honest, it's a health hazard.

Simon: (*sniggers*) Really? Mum doesn't cook much. She just microwaves stuff.

Janice: But the empty packets are everywhere. You could recycle some of it.

Simon: (*yawns*) Relax! You're doing my head in! Listen to the music. Why bother recycling? That means sorting stuff out. Can't be bothered. Isn't my job!

Janice: (*sniffs*) The lounge – it smells funny!

Simon: (*trying to put his arms around Janice, who swiftly moves away*) Ah the smell – well, you see the two Alsatians in the back garden?

Janice: (*hesitant*) Y – yes.

Simon: (*matter-of-fact*) Training them takes effort. So, they mess on the carpet. I made some time to clean it up before you came round.

Janice: (*disgusted*) Thanks a lot, Simon.

Simon: Glad you're appreciative 'cause (*yawns*) it took energy to clean it all up.

Janice: (*stands up*) Yuck!

Simon: (*tries to pull Janice back onto the settee*) What are you doing, Janice? Relax!

Janice: (*forceful*) I've learned a lesson. I now know where slothfulness leads to. I'm . . . I'm going back to school. Bye Simon!

If your students would like to act out this short play, they can get into groups of four and improvise a scene where Janice returns to school and discusses with Alice about how she will change her slothful ways from now on.

Envy by Carl Barton, Clarence Hayesmore and Tom Edgington

(*Tom, Carl and Clarence meet in the school playground.*)

Tom: (*to Carl and Clarence*) Guess what, I'm going in for the Mensa test next week.

Carl: (*not surprised*) Well, you did come top in every subject last year.

Clarence: Perhaps you'll break a Mensa record or something?

Tom: (*laughs in a good natured way*) I enjoy working hard and finding things out. It's like a hobby to me. (*glances at his watch*) Must go – got a practice match in the gym. The big footie game's on tomorrow. The Junior Cup Final! Hope we win!

(*Tom walks away, whistling.*)

Carl: (*to Clarence*) I wish I was as clever as Tom.

Clarence: (*downcast*) Makes you sick, doesn't he! He's annoying. He's popular, good at everything . . . including sport. I bet we win that Junior Cup because he'll score a double hat-trick or something.

Carl: (*laughs*) He's good at all the written stuff, he's good at sport and his mum and dad are mega rich. Because they're mega rich, he's got all the latest computer gadgets.

Clarence: Yeah, and he lives in the biggest house in our street. It's like a mansion, with a swimming pool.

Sam: (*Overhears conversation and sidles up to the friends*) Hi mates – how you both doin' then? Talkin' 'bout Tom. Annoying ain't he?

Clarence/Carl: Yeah!

Sam: (*cheerful*) Tom's good at anything, can do everything, owns almost everything. Have I summed him up right or have I not? Makes you envious, eh?

Carl: Yeah, all you say . . . that just about sums things up.

Sam: Envy, eh? Terrible thing is envy.

Clarence: (*shrugs his shoulders*) It'd be good to have some of what he's got.

Carl: Yeah!

Sam: (*scowls*) We need to bring him down a peg or two.

Clarence: (*surprised*) What do you mean?

Sam: If you really want Thomas brought down a peg or two, then it shall be done.

Carl: (*enthusiastic*) How?

(*The playground suddenly becomes windy and the wind seems to howl and moan, like a lost soul.*)

Sam: (*producing a parchment from his jacket pocket*) Just sign this paper. (*sees Clarence and Carl hesitate*) Just a tease, a joke mates!

Clarence: (*reads parchment*) We the undersigned agree that we are full of envy for Thomas Edington. We agree to do him harm because we are envious. By signing this document, we agree to allow S. A. Tan to wreck Thomas Edington's life. By signing this document we surrender our souls to the said Samuel A. Tan in twenty years' time. Signed Clarence Haysmore and Carl Barton (*gives parchment back to Sam*). That's all a bit strong!

Carl: Didn't know you had a middle name, Sam.

Sam: Middle name, Mates. Yeah – it's Anthony – but don't let on (*speaking quietly*). This (*indicating parchment*) is our little secret, eh mates? (*to himself*) The document will only work if Tom hates them for what they do. Come on mates, want to join the joke or what? It's only a bit of fun, remember!

(*Clarence and Carl sign the parchment. Sam is smiling as he folds the parchment back inside his jacket pocket.*)

Be seein' you mates – got to dash; got other souls to . . . eh, other jobs to do.

Clarence: (*to Carl*) I don't think we should have signed that document. It might be binding in some way.

(*The following day at school. The class are sitting at their desks in the form room.*)

Mr Guest: Glad you are all here today. I have rather bad news for you all (*coughs*). Poor Thomas Edington can't play in the Junior Cup Final as he broke his leg yesterday during the practice match.

(*Carl and Clarence exchange nervous glances.*)

By a bizarre coincidence, his parent's house burned down – some say – due to an undetected electrical fault. His dad's business collapsed and the house was uninsured. So, I'm afraid poor Tom has lost everything.

Carl: (*bitter*) We got our wish, Clarence.

Clarence: (*worried*) And we signed the document.

Carl: See where envy has got us.

Clarence: Let's tell Tom everything. We need to admit his bad luck is all our fault.

(*A week later, Carl and Clarence meet Tom in his temporary home. They tell him the whole story.*)

Tom: (*he is his usual cheerful self*) So – you repent of your sin of envy?

Carl/Clarence: Yes, we do.

Tom: (*serious*) There are some things in life more important than stuff. As my dad always says, there are no pockets in a shroud. I'm not disappointed that I've lost everything. Why? Because I've gained you two as real friends.

Carl/Clarence: We'll be your true friends forever!

Tom: Sam Anthony Tan can stay away from us all – he can't harm us!

Carl: (*puzzled*) The strange thing is, I haven't seen him about since your mishaps, Tom.

Tom: (*confident*) You won't see him again. He was seen, with some weird friends of his, running from my house just before the fire started. He's in serious trouble. I believe a special place is reserved for him, where he'll stay for the rest of his days.

If your students wish, they could act this short play out and write a further scene where Sam is trying to tempt somebody else.

CHAPTER 8

Drama across the curriculum

The value of drama across the curriculum

Whatever subject you teach, drama can be a useful learning tool. It allows students to work in a meaningful context and they become actively involved in their own learning. They can also express themselves emotionally. Working through drama allows your students to build self-confidence – thereby reducing discipline problems. Students can transfer skills learned in drama lessons. Drama enables your students to explore creative ways in which to express and communicate their ideas and opinions. They can also work collaboratively, building on each other's ideas. Most of all, as I wrote in my introduction (page 2), tell me and I will forget; show me and I will remember; involve me and I will understand. The work suggested below only scratches the surface of all that could be done to introduce drama into every subject lesson. My hope is that subject specialists will seize the opportunity to produce better subject-specific material than I have done here.

Drama and citizenship/PSHE

Citizenship/PSHE lessons can be enhanced by the use of drama within these lessons. Students can learn a great deal through role play.

During the course of a year, you are likely to cover bullying in some form or another – possibly with a Year 7 group. Many schools will have their own or a county anti-bullying policy. It will usually state somewhere that bullying will not be tolerated – in any form. For the following work, ask your students the question, what is bullying? They will probably identify some or all of the following points;

Name calling/malicious gossip/teasing
Physical bullying
Written or verbal threats
Bullying with a racial motive/class motive
Text message/email or chat room site bullying

Here is what Childline says about bullying:

What is bullying?
Bullying can mean many different things.

These are some ways children and young people have described bullying:

being called names
being teased
being pushed or pulled about
having money and other possessions taken or messed about with
having rumours spread about you
being ignored and left out
being hit, kicked or physically hurt in any way
being threatened or intimidated

Bullying can also be part of other forms of abuse, including neglect, emotional, physical and sexual abuse.

If you are being bullied in person or online, then you might think that it's your fault. It isn't.

No-one has the right to bully you. If you speak out about it, there are people who care – they will listen to you and help you.

*   *   *

Ask your students to form groups of four or five and get them to discuss what it feels like to be bullied. Then ask them to think of ways in which bullying could be stopped.

Then ask your students to improvise a situation where a student is bullied in some way. They need to thought shower ideas, looking at the five points above.

Tell your students that there must be a positive outcome. They can look at the Childline advice about how to tackle bullying for a realistic ending to their improvisation.

Advice from Childline
The best way to protect yourself from being bullied is to tell someone so that you can get some help. If you try to fight back, you might make the situation worse or get into trouble yourself.

Here are some other ideas about how you can deal with bullying. Think about your situation, and what options might be best for you.

- Don't ignore bullying – it won't go away on its own and it may get worse.
- Tell someone you trust – such as a teacher, parent or friend.
- Remember – it's not your fault. No one deserves to be bullied.

Here are some other things you might want to think about:

- Keep a record – and save any nasty texts or emails that you have been sent.
- If possible try to stay away from the bullies or stay with a group when you don't feel safe.
- Ask your mates to look out for you.
- Try not to fight back – you could get into trouble or get hurt.
- Check your school's anti-bullying policy. This will tell you what your school should do about bullying.

For a further activity – ask your students to imagine that they wish to set up their own anti-bullying committee. Their intention is to interview bullied students and those that do the bullying. They have to present their ideas to the head teacher and two school governors. One of the school governors has a daughter at the school who is a victim of bullying.

In groups of about four or five, ask your students to decide who will act the role of a head teacher, a chair of governors, a parent governor and the students who are presenting their ideas.

Your students now need to role play the scenario.

Should you wish to take the bulling theme further, students can access ideas from the following internet sites; www.antibullying-week.co.uk, www.anti-bullyingalliance.org.uk, www.kidscape.org.uk, www.beatbullying.co.uk, and www.bullybusters.org.uk.

Here is a short scenario about bullying with some following activities.

'The Project'

*(Nihal, Charmaine and Guy are discussing the wildlife project that
   Miss Tydeman, the Science Teacher, has set for homework.)*

Nihal: Got the homework sussed, Charmaine?

Charmaine: *(sarcastic)* Yeah, sure! With **my** social life I've got loads of time to find out about British wildlife!

Guy: *(listening)* Haven't made a start yet – guess we'll all be in **big** trouble with Miss Tydeman.

Charmaine: *(thinking)* Unless – I know a geek who's probably worked hard on this project. He's probably done it all! You know who I mean?

Nihal/Guy: Chuck Fawsett.

Charmaine: (*laughing*) The very person.

(*Later, in a dark corner of the playground, Chuck is confronted by the bullies.*)

Guy: (*soothing voice*) So then Chuck, what have you done on the wildlife project so far?

Chuck: (*innocent*) I've worked on amphibians.

Guy: (*confused*) Am-what-ians?

Chuck: (*enthusiastic*) You know Guy; toads, frogs and the different types of newts.

Guy: (*still confused*) Oh yeah . . . whatever!

Nihal: (*getting closer to Chuck in a way that appears menacing*) Interesting! What else?

Chuck: (*trying to move away*) I've written a page on the black grouse and . . . (*thinking*) a couple of pages on the re-introduction of the hazel dormouse and, oh yeah, . . . say, why are you three so interested in **my** project?

Charmaine: (*threatening*) 'Cause it's soon going to be *our* project.

Nihal: So, wimp, hand over!

Guy: (*shows a bunched fist*) Or you're dead meat.

Nihal: Dead meat, squinty eyes.

Charmaine: (*laughs in a nasty way*) Or we'll text your mates and tell them what you *really* think of them. Perhaps we'll spread rumours on your chat sites.

Guy: (*thumping Chuck in the stomach, hard enough for Chuck to wince in pain*) Give us the project now.

Chuck: (*gasping for breath*) I – don't-carry-it-around-with-me.

Guy: (*unconcerned*) So – run and get it, cretin. Or you'll know what's coming your way.

(*The bullies laugh as Chuck runs off.*)

Ask your students to work in groups of four and act out the scenario. They should then re-read the advice from Childline and work out what different types of bullying the three bullies employ to intimidate Chuck.

Allow your students to thought tunnel Chuck and whisper to him how he might be feeling at this point in time. Then ask them to hot seat one of the bullies and/or Chuck, and ask them questions concerning the scenario. Get them to discover why they acted as they did and ask them to discuss their intended future actions.

Finally, ask your students to write a conclusion to the play. The conclusion must be a positive outcome for Chuck.

One of the most inventive conclusions achieved by my students during this activity was a con trick devised by Chuck. He re-wrote the project using animals that did not exist, but seemed believable and gave the wrong information about such animals as the polecat. He handed in a correct project but gave the bullies the false one. They were all given a hefty detention for wrong information and for copying (they all handed in the same project). When they tried to blame Chuck, they were in serious trouble for bullying!

Your students may wish to use Childline advice as a basis for their play ending.

Fair and unfair

Ask your students to work in pairs and discuss what they see as fair and unfair. They could focus on some interesting issues such as;

- Are boys and girls/women and men/treated equally?
- Is a person who uses a wheelchair treated equal to somebody who does not use a wheelchair?
- Are people with different religious beliefs (or with religious beliefs) treated fairly?
- Is the voting system fair?
- Is the law fair?
- Is there a class system in our country? If so, is it fair?

Your students can add ideas of their own. They should then form groups of four or five and look at one area that they feel unfairness exists. They should then consider how they might make an impact. They might consider some of the following points –

- Vote for a political party that shares their views. (When old enough to do so)
- Joining a political party.
- Write to their M.P.
- Form a pressure group.

Remaining in their groups, students should consider a school issue that they would like to change. For example, they may feel that there is nowhere for their particular year group to go during their lunch break when the weather is poor. They might consider the following points;

- Identifying an area within the school premises that could, with some alterations, become their common room.
- Write or speak to other members of their year group, to gain support for the idea.
- Meet their head of year to discuss why they feel they need a common room.
- Write to the head teacher and school governors for support.

Now ask your students to role play the talk between their chosen student representatives and their head of year. They should then role play a situation where their student representatives meet the head teacher, the chair of governors and a parent governor, to try and persuade the adults to agree to their proposal.

Tip: Your students will need to research and write down the practicalities such as – what is the designated area used for now? How can it be transformed into a common room. How will the common room be 'policed' to make sure it is a safe environment that remains vandal-free. What are the cost implications? How will money be raised for items such as comfortable chairs? Who will redecorate the area to make sure it is student friendly. When will this be done and how? Will there be a student committee to make sure the area is left clean and tidy after break has finished?

For those students who are role playing the head teacher or a governor, the above questions (and some of their own) could be used.

For an extra activity, students could take on an issue they feel is unfair. For example, they might feel that some countries are rich and others are very poor (or there is a wealth difference in Britain. Some parts of Britain are rich, other parts are poor). They should discuss what could be done to make things fairer. This activity must lead to a role-play situation. For example, taking the idea above – role play a committee on social equality. There should be a chairperson, a proposer (who is for the idea of social equality) can suggest that wealth and jobs are diverted to a poorer area of the country. New hospitals and schools could be built in that area as well as new industrial complexes. The speaker against social equality could suggest that the poor area became poor due to industrial unrest and strikes in the 1960s and to divert money to this area would be a disaster.

Rights and responsibilities
Ask your students to look at the following statements.

'I have the right to do whatever I like. Nobody can stop me!' Tasmin.

'Why should I be responsible for walking and feeding my pet dog? That's an adult's job. Dad can do it.' Adojan.

'Nobody should have any rights unless they accept responsibilities,' Pembe.

'The government should find everyone a job. My dad's unemployed and it isn't fair,' Matt.

'Everybody has the right to a happy and fulfilled life,' Eluned.

Ask your students to work in pairs and discuss which statements they agree with and which statements they think are wrong. They need to say why they agree/disagree with the statements.

Now ask your students to form groups of about four or five and discuss the question, what are rights and what rights should everyone have? They might come up with some of the following –

- The right to express opinions.
- The right to worship in freedom.
- The right to privacy.
- The right to be different.

Then ask your students if they think every society has allowed people to have rights. Remind them that Nazi Germany took away individual rights from some people and from some ethnic groups. Ask them why do we have asylum seekers and should they have an automatic right to citizenship in our country?

Now ask your students to mime a situation where someone's rights have been infringed in some way. It might be the right to be physically unharmed or it could be the right to vote in a country that has a dictator. When a group has mimed a situation, those watching can guess what that situation was portraying.

When the mimes are complete, ask your students to look at the issue below. This issue is the **right** to good health. This is linked to the **responsibility** you have to ensure that you do what you can to keep in good health.

Discussion/viewpoint

I have had success with this activity with both mixed ability key Stage Three students and with top set Key Stage Three students.

Allow your students to form themselves into groups of four. Tell them they are a committee of hospital surgeons of the near future. In this future world, money is short and doctors/surgeons are forced to decide who needs to be operated on. Which of the following four people would your students decide is the one who deserves the operation. The operation required is a hip replacement.

Patient One: Stuart Small (aged 53). He is twelve stone and six foot tall. He has no previous serious medical history. He claims to have smoked for most of his life and he is prone to fits of coughing. His blood pressure is high. He works as a plumber and claims he can't do his job if his hip isn't replaced. He owns his own business and, being off sick, is finding lack of money a real problem.

Patient Two: Graham Pigott. (aged 46). He is sixteen stone but only five foot three inches tall. He was recently diagnosed with diabetes and has been to various weight watchers courses. He claims he loves his food. He frequently snacks between meals, particularly when he is watching TV. He also suffers with asthma. He is unemployed and has not had a job for ten years.

Patient Three: Henry Chatfield (aged 78). He is tall but weighs under eleven stone. He knows hip replacements last for ten years and because he has no known medical problems, believes he will live that long. He was in the army and lost a foot when he stepped on a mine when in action. He still helps out at charity events, raising money for good causes. His blood pressure is low.

Patient Four: Sean Maloney (aged 60). He has just retired and worked in the building trade. He is just under ten stone and claims he drinks and smokes occasionally. He suffered a heart attack four years ago but appears to have made a full recovery. He lives alone but his children and grandchildren live near by.

Having read the case studies, your students should decide what information concerning each patient is relevant and which is not relevant. If they are stuck, point out that patient one has high blood pressure and he smokes. Should these facts be significant in their decision? Patient two is overweight and a diabetic (due to the fact that he is overweight) does he deserve to have the operation as he has not significantly dieted to help himself become fitter? Patient three is the oldest patient but does age matter ? Finally, is the fact that patient four suffered a heart attack of any significance?

Remind your students that they are looking at rights and responsibilities. Who do they think has the right to have the hip replacement and who has been the most responsible at trying to preserve their health?

Once a group has made their decision, allow the students to gather as a class. If they have all made different decisions, ask them to choose one member from each group to debate the issue. See if the class can arrive at a consensus view.

As a further activity, ask your students if they think doctors should ever have the right to decide who should have an operation and who should not.

Roles and identities

The following work is appropriate for students in Years 10 and 11.

Ask your students the question, what is a career? When they have understood that everyone should have a career, ask them to form into groups of four and to talk about their personal life plans. What career might they choose and how do they aim to get into that career – what qualifications do they need?

Now ask them to read through the job interviews.

The Job Interview

(Stuart is sitting outside a small office.)

Manager: Do come in! (*sees Stuart, who is dressed in old jeans and a denim jacket*) Do take a . . . oh!

Stuart: (*enters, takes a seat and slouches*) Good place this, innit? Like to 'ave your job!

Manager: (*ignores Stuart*) Now, you are applying for the position of trainee sales assistant in our company.

Stuart: (*sniffs*) Yeah, that's right, gov. Lots of dosh, eh?

Manager: Have you had any experience in this kind of work? Any relevant work experience, perhaps?

Stuart: (*shrugs his shoulders*) Dunno, really. Probably not, no.

Manager: Why did you apply for this particular position? (*Stuart remains silent*) Well, do you get on with people?

Stuart: (*thinking*) Yeah, think so, mate! But some of the snotty type of teachers don't like me. They think I'm trying to cause trouble. (*laughs*) Expect I do at times.

Manager: (*patient*) Being a sales assistant means being a good talker . . . and listener . . . being able to relate to people.

Stuart: Yeah . . . I get on fine with people outside school. In the clubs, with me mates, I'm the life and soul of the party; get my drift?

Manager: (*coughs*) So . . . what are your interests? (*silence*) You do have hobbies, don't you?

Stuart: (*enthusiastic*) I used to like football . . . nowadays, I mostly hang around town with me mates. We have a good laugh.

Interview Two: (The same small office)

(*A knock on the door.*)

Manager: Do come in! (*A smartly dressed boy enters and stands behind the empty seat. Manager gestures to the empty seat*) Do sit down.

Gavin: (*sits up straight and appears attentive*) Thank you.

Manager: Now, you are applying for the position of trainee sales assistant in our company.

Gavin: Yes, that's right.

Manager: Have you any experience in this kind of work? Any relevant work experience, perhaps?

Gavin: (*eager*) Yes. I worked in a care home for my school work experi- ence. I think I managed fine with the senior citizens. They were sorry to see me leave at the end of the fortnight. (*short pause*) I helped out in a small shop during the summer holidays.

Manager: I see. (*pause*) Why did you apply for this particular position?

Gavin: (*keen*) I enjoy working with people. At school, I was elected Year 11 representative for the School Council. I hear other students' ideas (*laughs*) and sometimes their complaints. Then I report back to the school senior managers. (*pause*) So I thought the kind of job offered would suit me.

Manager: (*interested*) Do you have any outside school interests?

Gavin: (*thinks*) Yes . . . I volunteer for community activities, such as
    making space for nature in our local park. My mum helps out at the
    Village Hall and I often serve the tea after events.
Manager: Now we should talk about . . .

Ask your students to imagine they are the manager of the company. Which of the two interviewees would they give the job to and why? After they have decided, ask them to split off into pairs and role play an interview for a job they would like. One takes the part of the manager, the other the interviewee. After a while, they can swap roles.

As a plenary session, ask your students to discuss how they managed in an interview situation. What went right, what went wrong and how could they improve.

Roles, identities and enterprise

Ask your students to work in groups of eight to ten. They should understand that business functions as a partnership of people who have different natural abilities and strengths. They will also have different skills and aptitudes. Working together, these different types of people can make a business become successful.

Your students should discuss what each of them has to offer in terms of natural strengths, skills and aptitudes. Ask your students to work on the idea of producing a school magazine that will make a profit. They will need to think of the following;

- Who will become the editor? The editor should be somebody the rest of the group can work with, so the editor's interpersonal skills need to be good.
- Who will write the articles? Do you liaise with the English department, so that some articles and stories will come from lesson-time activities?
- What should go into the magazine?
- How is this venture going to be financed? Is money going to be borrowed to get the venture going or is it possible to find sponsors? Is it possible to make up and sell adverts for local business?

Ask your students to look at the following questions and (perhaps) divide into smaller groups to take on particular areas.

As a further activity, why not turn theory into practice? Your students could produce a magazine and sell it to other year groups. Why not involve interested teachers and parents? In my experience as a teacher, the most difficult area for students is to recon up the financial implications – such as printing costs. They also need to decide who will type the articles. The students whom I gave this task to and who produced the best magazine did involve local businesses for sponsor money and sold the idea of advertising for local companies. They succeeded in attracting business. The magazine was sold in advance to fellow students and to parents during parent consultation evenings. This group went on to produce a book, with the help of an established author! It can be done!

Our students need to consider **risk**, which is necessary in business – but the risk factors need to be assessed. For example, will the product sell? Students should discuss this factor and try to obtain advance sales. However, by doing so they need to be confident that they can deliver a good product. The book produced by my Year 10 class sold out because they had chosen a topic that would interest most younger students and parents. It was a book of collected ghost stories. They collected the stories!

Prejudice

Ask your students if they think the definition below is correct. How might they change the definition?

Definition: Prejudice is a pre-judgement about someone or something before having full knowledge to be able to make a fair judgement.

In groups of about four, ask your students to look at the areas of prejudice below. Do they agree with the wording and, if not, how would they change the wording?

- **Racism** – is an attitude towards some races because of the colour of their skin or the language they speak. It is the belief that some races are inferior. This attitude can lead to ethnic cleansing.
- **Sexism** – is the belief that one sex is inferior to another. In the past men had the power to decide what life women had and some men wanted their wives to stay at home. Girls , in Victorian times, did not receive the same education as boys.
- **Religious prejudice** – some people who have no religious belief can be prejudiced against those who have a religious belief.
- **Social** – some people are prejudiced against those from another social class, because of the way they speak or because they hold different values.
- **Ageism** – Young and old people can be subject to prejudice due to their age. Young people can see older people as 'past it' with nothing to offer. On the other hand, older people can think all youngsters are 'up to no good'.

Ask your students to add to the five areas of prejudice listed above. They should be able to think of at least three areas of prejudice in our society.

Still in their groups, your students should look again at ageism. Ask them to read the two short plays. Having read the first play, ask them to use their experiences to decide how probable is the scenario portrayed in the play. Ask them; 'Is it realistic or just a stereotype of perceived prejudices?' This should be suitable for key stage three students.

At The Supermarket

(A number of people are shopping at the supermarket on a busy Saturday afternoon.)

Mrs Grumble: *(sees Mr Grouse and leaves her trolley in the middle of the aisle to speak to him)* Hello, Mr Grouse, how are you these cold winter days?

Mr Grouse: *(rolls his eyes up to heaven)* Old age isn't for wimps. What with my arthritis and my bad back . . .

(Three young girls carefully push the trolley to one side, so they can squeeze past.)

Mrs Grumble: Did you see that, Mr Grouse? Flighty girls up to no good! Today's young people, they aren't like we were in the glorious good old days.

Mr Grouse: *(watches the girls pass him)* Oh no. They wear very little clothing – and those bare midriffs, wonder they aren't all taken ill with pneumonia. No respect for their elders and betters, either.

Mrs Grumble: No manners, that's what the trouble is. Don't know what they're taught at the school these days.

(She grabs her trolley and swings it into the legs of young Martin Davids.) Out of my way, boy!

Mr Grouse: Yes, out of her way!

Martin: *(rubbing his shins)* That hurt. You're not going to say sorry for bumping into me?

Mr Grouse: (angry) Cheeky young so-and-so!

Now ask your students to read the following short play and discuss how realistic is the situation portrayed in the play.

Life saver

(A group of young people are gathered in Craig's parents' house. They are about to play their guitars.)

Rory: I hate our music teacher, he's old . . . he's decrepit. He can't teach us anything.

Jane: *(calm)* He has a wealth of experience, Rory.

Rory: *(ignoring Jane)* Old people ought to be done away with – got rid of.

Craig: (*enthusiastic*) Yeah. I mean, what good are they to anyone. They're all clapped-out has-beens.

Rory: (*fiddles with his guitar*) Anyone over the age of seventy ought to be given some sort of lethal injection.

Lucy: (*very enthusiastic*) Euthanasia, great idea! The country would save tons of money. No pensions to pay out and our health service could look after people that really matter – us!

Jane: (*annoyed*) Nerd brains, all of you. Of course old people have a lot to offer. My Grandma . . .

(*Martha bursts into the room, breathless*)

Martha: (*hands to her sides*) Have you heard about old Mr Kenway and Rory's dad? (*spots Rory*) Oh . . . so you can't know!

Rory: (*strums his guitar*) Has old Kenway done something useful . . . like die!

Martha: (*glances at Rory with pity in her eyes*) No, he hasn't died. (*quietly*) He's just saved your dad's life!

Rory: (*places his guitar firmly against the table*) What do you mean?

Martha: (*still trying to catch her breath*) Your dad was drilling . . .

Rory: (*interrupting*) Yeah, he was putting up some shelving for mum.

Martha: He drilled through an electrical cable. Your mum found him and thought he was dead. Mr Kenway might be over eighty, but he knows a thing or two about resuscitation. Old Kenway saved your dad's life, Rory.

Jane: (*firm*) So you see, Rory, not all old people are useless!

In their groups, your students can decide who are the characters in the plays that show their prejudices and what are their prejudices. They can then take it in turn to counsel the characters they consider to exhibit prejudiced thoughts and actions.

Drama and English

Drama and English go well together. There are many drama activities that can be useful for English students. Students often have difficulty understanding poetry, so I often use drama activities to support students' understanding of poetry. The poem below is complex and suitable for AS/A Level students.

'The World' by Henry Vaughan

I saw Eternity the other night
Like a great Ring of pure and endless light
   All calm as it was bright;
And round beneath it, Time, in hours, days, years,
   Driven by the spheres,
Like a vast shadow moved, in which the world

And all her train were hurled.
The doting Lover in his quaintest strain
    Did there complain;
Near him, his lute, his fancy, and his flights,
    Wit's sour delights;
With gloves and knots, the silly snares of pleasure;
    Yet his dear treasure
All scattered lay, while he his eyes did pour
    Upon a flower.

The darksome Statesman hung with weights and woe,
Like a thick midnight fog, moved there so slow
    He did nor stay nor go;
Condemning thoughts, like sad eclipses, scowl
    Upon his soul,
And clouds of crying witnesses without
    Pursued him with one shout.
Yet digged the mole, and, lest his ways be found,
    Worked under ground,
Where he did clutch his prey; but One did see
    That policy.
Churches and altars fed him, perjuries
    Were gnats and flies;
It rained about him blood and tears, but he
    Drank them as free.

The fearful Miser on a heap of rust
Sat pining all his life there, did scarce trust
    His own hands with the dust;
Yet would not place one piece above, but lives
    In fear of thieves.
Thousands there were as frantic as himself,
    And hugged each one his pelf.
The downright Epicure placed heaven in sense
    And scorned pretence;
While others, slipped into a wide excess,
    Said little less;
The weaker sort, slight, trivial wares enslave,
    Who think them brave;
And poor despisèd Truth sat counting by
    Their victory.

Yet some, who all this while did weep and sing,
And sing and weep, soared up into the Ring;
    But most would use no wing.
'Oh, fools,' said I, 'thus to prefer dark night

> Before true light,
> To live in grots and caves, and hate the day
> Because it shows the way,
> The way which from this dead and dark abode
> Leaps up to God,
> A way where you might tread the sun, and be
> More bright than he.'
> But as I did their madness so discuss,
> One whispered thus,
> *This Ring the Bridegroom did for none provide*
> *But for his Bride.*

Ask your students to work in pairs and read the poem to each other, perhaps taking a verse each. They may want to make brief notes when making their first decisions as to what the poem is about.

Then ask your students to work in groups of four. They could then improvise the first verse, giving the poem their own dramatic interpretation. For example, the lover could be playing his lute while his girlfriend lies beside him. Note that she is refusing him. It is unrequited love! Some students might think she is dead!

Looking at the second verse, ask your students what they think the statesman (politician) is doing. Is he in Hell or condemning himself for what he has done in this life? Is he compared to a mole because he has dark secrets and 'condemning thoughts'? Ask your students to improvise the scene representing the statesman.

The third verse concentrates on the wrong attitudes of a miser. Ask your students to act out a scenario with the miser and his 'heap of rust'. Can they understand what the poet is telling us about misers?

The final verse gives us an insight into the poet's thoughts. They appear to be that most people will prefer sin to holiness. Only the bride (Christ's church of true believers) will get to heaven. Tell your students that Henry Vaughan lived from 1622–1695. Have attitudes and beliefs changed since then? Ask them if they are able to improvise this final verse?

Now, ask your students to put all the verses together and improvise a continuous piece.

For the teacher: 'The World', a brief summary.

'**The World**' is made up of four fifteen-line stanzas (I have called them verses for student ease). The stanzas are in a complex rhythm.

1) Iambic pentameter. 2) Iambic pentameter. 3) Iambic trimeter. 4) Iambic pentameter. 5) Iambic dimeter. 6) Iambic pentameter. 7) Iambic trimeter. 8) Iambic pentameter. 9) Iambic dimeter. 10) Iambic pentameter. 11) Iambic dimeter. 12) Iambic pentameter. 13) Iambic dimeter. 14) Iambic pentameter. 15) Iambic dimeter. The rhyme scheme is aaa, bb, cc, dd, ee, ff and gg.

The title is ambiguous (deliberately so) in that it reflects the dual focus of the poem – which is that the earthly world (of the here and now) is contrasted with the world to come for believers – and is heaven/eternity. Also, the world is the physical globe (line 6) of life here and now and of the future/eternity.

The four stanzas develop Vaughan's idea (although not specifically stated, he implies) that unless we shed our concern for worldly values, pleasures and deeds, we will be doomed to a lost eternity.

Ask your students to read through the poem again. They might like to consider various techniques they could use, that they might have learned in drama. For example, can they use a freeze frame for effect? (pages 25 and 30). Could some of the action benefit from mime techniques (pages 39 and 69) while a student reads part of the poem?

To reinforce understanding of the poem, do the groups want to hot seat (page 35) 'Henry Vaughan' to ask questions about the poem? For some groups, you the teacher could be Henry Vaughan. Would cross-cutting (page 38) be appropriate, to reorder the sequence of the poem? Perhaps students could begin their improvisation with the final verse? Would music or sound cues (pages 42 and 77) enhance the understanding of the poem?

For a **further activity**, students could turn the poem into a play. I have often found this idea a useful tool to enhance understanding. Below is how a pair of students turned the poem into a play. It is not necessarily a correct understanding of the poem but will raise discussion points. It also gives the teacher an idea of the level of understanding that your students have for the poem. After your students have written and performed their plays, you can have a general discussion about the issues raised in the plays.

'*The World*' by Henry Vaughan
(play version by Ruth Potter and Carol Skeir)
Narrator One: I saw eternity the other night.
Narrator Two: Like a great ring of pure and endless light.
Narrator Three: All calm as it was bright.
Narrator Four: Driven by the spheres.
Lover: All this world moves like a vast shadow. I just want to be rid of this world. (*throws down his lute*) I admit, I want her. She does not seem to want me. Perhaps she likes other people better than me. Or perhaps she'll never know a man – and grow old and die, like a flower in a field.
Devil: (*glancing at girl*) She'll never be yours unless you take her!
Lover: (*looks sorrowfully at the girl*) There she is, at the height of her beauty. (*picks a flower*) She'll be like this flower, withered and gone. Within days this flower will be withered and my lover will, one day, become just dry bones, her flesh picked by the scavenger birds. (*he*

    observes the flower) How colourful is this flower, how distracting! But
    it will wither and perish!
  Devil: (*laughs*) Decay – it's the way of all mankind.

Please note: This play is an interpretation of the poem and not necessarily the correct interpretation. It would, though, form an interesting group discussion concerning the meaning of the poem.

For a further look at how drama can help the understanding of poetry, ask your students to read the poem below. I have done this activity with key stage three and key stage four students.

Past Sounds
Through crackling firewood
Old man heard voices – calling,
Cackling, dim, distant
Past sounds–

Like scuffling rat's feet
Upon cracked tiles,

Like soldier's bodies
Stiff, upon the battlefield.

Like his mother's voice
Long ago beckoning . . .
Calling him home.

Flames of youth,
Times of songs in cold stone churches,
Sadness beside a white tomb.

All die into embers,
Of solitude.

Passion, too, dies a special, dismal death
For most.

New avenues of warm exploration
Become roadways without end.

Become dust,
Boredom,
Distain.

Life that once sizzled
And burned brightly
Becomes so trite
The weary traveller
Loses his way,
Forgets his balance . . .

And discovers he is staring into
Dying embers,
Listening to past sounds.

Sean Casey

Your students can be inventive with this poem. An idea that I tried and the students enjoyed, was to get them to turn the poem into a series of snapshots, while one student narrates the poem. Here is how it was done;

First snapshot: An old man is warming his hands by an open fire. (*We had fire crackling sound effects.*) Voices call him – for instance;
'My son, where are you going? Your home is here, not in the army.'
'Don't leave me on this battlefield to die, Johnny.'
(*Please note, we decided to call the person Johnny, although he is not given a name in the poem.*)
The narrator reads the first part of the poem **after** the words are spoken by the 'voices'.
Second snapshot: 'Johnny' embraces a young lady. They hug. An arch-way is formed by other students for 'Johnny' and his bride to walk through. Confetti is thrown.
Third Snapshot: 'Johnny' is sitting beside a white tomb. He is holding a bunch of flowers. Slow, gloomy music is played.
Fourth Snapshot: 'Johnny', now middle-aged, is drinking from a bottle. He is looking at a road. (We used a wide busy road, with signs as a backdrop. The signs had writing such as 'Drugs this way', 'Thieving, two years' and so on.)
Fifth Snapshot: 'Johnny' dressed in rags, has a stick over his shoulder, carrying his worldly goods, Dick Whittington style.
Sixth Snapshot: This is a repeat of the first snapshot.

Working in groups of about four or five, your students should be able to put their own interpretation on the poem, making up their own series of snapshots.

As an extra activity, they might like to take it in turns to hot seat the old man.

Here are two poems for younger students.

'No Homework'

There's a club,
in our school
and I'm a member.

It's the no homework club!

We stay late,
when the ghosts of the day

have entered the room . . .
blowing sweet paper
and crisp packets
across the cold floor.

We sit, desks apart,
thinking of writing,
calculating
doing sums,
writing paragraphs
we should have
managed at home.

But my dad,
whisky-drunk,
shouts at mum
and I hide
in the neon-lit streets
watching cars
and shoppers
Wend their way homeward.

Later, with chip-greasy fingers,
I stare at the theatre goers;
the boozers and bashers –
before I slink back home,
to mum's tears and bruises

I'm best attendee at the homework club.

Keith West

Younger students, possibly Years 7 and/or 8 might be able to tackle the work below.

The intention is for them to do a similar activity to the work achieved by older students, who made snapshots from 'Past Sounds'.

Maths Lesson

Enter the gut-twisting,
heart-thumping, brow-beating
dream-fear inducing
slum of a room.

There stands Mr Matthews,
Mighty Caesar of maths.
Him of the grey-balding head
And pig-ears and fag smelling breath.

His nicotine fingers hold
Chalk that fragments into dust
Like my fog-brain.

A nuclear warhead explodes
Somewhere in the centre of
My textbook and I'm dragged
Screaming and shouting
Down my failed days
To once again count
The slow tick of the grand clock
When the maths lesson
Seemed like a life sentence.

Paula Shuttleworth

Looking at 'No Homework'

This work is appropriate for Years 7 and 8. Your students can try a similar activity to that which was set for 'Past Sounds'. Your students can present 'No Homework' as a series of snapshots, using a narrator. Below is a suggestion of how it could be achieved.

Snapshot One: The No Homework Club is in operation. Several students are sitting behind their desks, looking at a textbook. A teacher is at the front of the class.

Snapshot Two: Dad and mum are at home. Perhaps dad has just struck mum, who is rubbing her cheek with her hand. An empty bottle lies on the floor. A boy is watching from a distance.

Snapshot Three: The boy is watching shoppers. For this, several students could be carrying bags.

Snapshot Four: Mum is comforted by her son. A broken bottle lies near by.

Snapshot Five: As snapshot one.

I am sure that your students, working in groups of about four or five, will be able to create their own imaginative snapshot.

Maths lesson

Allow your Year 7 or 8 students to read the poem to themselves. They should then find themselves in groups of four or five and think of inventive ways in which they can present the poem as a piece of drama. What techniques might they use? As a lighting technique, could they uplift (page 80) Mr Matthews? Could they block in (page 98) or face out (page 98). Might a noise collage (page 99) be appropriate? Here is an example.

'Maths Lesson' (The Play Version) by Siobhan Williams and Lucinda Graves

Matt: (*to Lucinda*) I used to like maths but I hate it now!

Lucinda: Mr Matthews is frightening. He's made the subject scary.

Mr Matthews: (*shouting*) Come along, you two . . . don't keep me waiting. We haven't got all day! Look at the whiteboard when you've found a seat.

Lucinda: (*stomach growls*) Oh no!

Mr Matthews: You'll see questions I've put up from the work we did last week.

Siobhan: (*coughs*) Oh no!

Mr Matthews: (*glares at Siobhan*) No coughing, no noise. Just get on with the work!

Siobhan: (*whispers to Lucinda*) I can't do this!

Lucinda: (*whispers back to Siobhan*) I feel sick!

Noise Collage: My guts feel like they're twisting inside me. This is a slum of a room. Thinks he's the mighty Caesar of maths. Horrible man. Grey, balding head – ugly. He's got pig ears. Fag smelling breath. Want to escape this dream-fear room.

(The above was the start of the play improvisation.)

Your students will be inventive and creative with this exercise and will produce their own interpretation.

Dealing at the market place

This is an exercise that I found useful for revising 'Macbeth' with a Year 9, 10 or 11 group. I have used this for Key Stage Three and Four, depending upon when 'Macbeth' is taught.

Allocate students into groups of three. Place desks at various points in the classroom. Make the room appear like a market place with stalls. Each member of the group should be given a different colour felt pen. I used blue, green and red, as distinctive colours. Now give each group of three a large piece of plain paper.

Tell your students they are about to be tested and a test will take place during the course of this exercise. Write the timing of each stage on the board. For your purposes, this is a revision exercise and not an exam question for the students to tackle.

Write: Stage One. Answer the question, 'Who was responsible for the death of King Duncan and what were the consequences?' Allow your students thinking time of about five minutes.

Write: Stage Two. You are all given part of an answer to this question. You will need to design a poster that members of the other groups will be able to view. The poster can only have a maximum number of twenty words. However – drawings, cartoons, symbols and sketches are to be used. Allow your students fifteen minutes to design their posters.

Write: Stage Three. Each group can choose one member of the group to stay at home as the stallholder. The other two members need to visit the market place and trade information with the other groups. They need to take notes as they read and work out what the other posters are telling them. Allow ten minutes for these negotiations.

Write: Stage Four. The two students now return to their stall and tell the other member and each other what information they have gleaned from the other stallholders. If a group is stuck, they are allowed to run back to another stall and have a quick look at their poster. Allow ten minutes for this exercise.

Write: Stage Five. Ask your students to place all their notes and the posters to one side. Now they are given the test – to make a plan to answer the written question on the board (Stage One). Allow ten minutes for your students to work out their plan.

Stage Six: *(Note – your students should not be aware that there is a stage six, so it should not be written on the board.)* Allow the groups to come together. You need the class to have all the accurate information as a revision exercise, so use this as a plenary session or a question and answer session. Make sure they (or you) go over all the points and that nothing is misunderstood.

Before you begin Stage Two.

For the exercise, give each market stall one piece of paper. There are at least seven possible pieces to make up the essay. If you have a class of over twenty-one, some groups may need to be in fours.

For this particular exercise, you could divide the answers up as follows;

- Nobody is fully responsible for the death of Duncan – although Macbeth actually killed the King.
- The witches – they tricked Macbeth by telling him some truths and encouraged him to go one stage further (King hereafter).
- Lady Macbeth – sometimes seen as the fourth witch, cajoled Macbeth into committing the murder.
- Banquo – he failed to tell anyone about the meeting with the witches; was this because he was told that his own son would be king one day?
- Macbeth – he was a fierce warrior (from the nave to the chaps) and he was ambitious, which was why he listened to the witches.

- King Duncan – he was foolish to put his trust into this Thane of Cawdor and said of the former, 'he was a gentleman in whom I put an absolute trust.' His understanding of other's motives was weak. Should he have named his son (Malcolm) as King?
- Consequences – Macbeth becomes King of Scotland and orders the death of Banquo. His kingship ruins Scotland. He orders the deaths of Macduff's wife and children. Lady Macbeth suffers madness and dies. Macbeth is eventually killed by Macduff.

Your students might be able to add other people as responsible for the death of Duncan. They can mention anything else during the plenary session.

For a variety: Instead of drawing posters, the stallholders could take it in turn to mime their part of the answer.

You can adapt the idea to the play and/or book you are studying with a particular group. However, this should be a one-off lesson and not tried too often.

Wheel of fortune

Play the game as a revision exercise. You will first of all need a few wheel of fortune boards. Split your groups into fours and ask them to follow the instructions below.

You will need to supply cardboard, scissors, pieces of brad (try asking your obliging technology teaching colleague. It worked for me!).

First of all, ask your students to draw a 12-inch round circle on a piece of cardboard. To draw the circle, they can either use a compass or trace a circle shape. They should then cut out the circle with a pair of scissors. Your students should then draw a vertical line down the centre of their circle. They then draw a horizontal line across the centre of their circle. They should continue to draw lines to delineate the sections on the board. As a reference, they should think about cutting a large pie into slices, but make the slices considerably thinner than an average apple pie slice! This means that they will have a lot of options when spinning the wheel. Ask them to colour the sections in the individual colours of their choice. Then, outline each section in black so the separation between the sections is easy to see. They then need to label each section with a number. Each number should be given a point amount. Be sure to vary your point options from space to space, don't group similar point amounts closely together. For example, place 9 next to 2 and so on. The number and the point amounts can be the same! They then need to draw an arrow on their piece of card. Now they should cut out the arrow and colour in as they wish. They should place the arrow pointing out from the centre of their game board and attach it into place by piercing a metal brad through the arrow and the game board. To spin the wheel, your students will flick the arrow to see where it lands.

To play the game, your students need to spin their wheel. When it lands on a number, they need to answer the question on that number. You supply the questions!

When I have played this game, I have given easy questions to students landing on a number one and a very difficult question for those landing on a number ten! For example, should you be revising 'Millions' an easy question might be, 'What is the name of Damian's brother? (Anthony). A more difficult question might be, 'Who was the martyr of Uganda? (St Charles Lwanga). You will need about thirty questions at your disposal. However, you can use the same questions for each group of four.

This game works for Key Stage Three students, for those revising GCSE and I have also used it with A and A/S English groups. It works very well with younger students as a spelling test. Easy spellings for those landing on a low number, harder spellings for those landing on a high number.

For bonus points of up to eight extra points, I have (if time allows) asked them to improvise a scene from the book studied, which relates to a question. For example, in 'Millions' can they show Damien and Anthony wallpapering Anthony's room with old money?

The game is meant to be competitive and the group who scores the most points at the end of the lesson wins. It is also a good way to revise work . . . which reinforces learning in an interesting way.

Information hunt

Before a lesson starts, hide pieces of paper all around the room, with lines from a poem (rhyming couplets) on the piece of paper. The students need to find the papers and place them together, working out how the poem is constructed. Use coloured paper and split your class into groups of four. The first group to logically reconstruct the poem wins! It is possible that the poem is not reconstructed as the poet wrote it – there might be valid alternatives. However, this fact leads you on to the next part of your lesson . . . a discussion on what is a poem. You can then continue the lesson asking your students to keep in their groups and decide what the poem is about.

For this exercise, I use a pre-twentieth-century poem such as 'The Mistletoe Bough' by Thomas Haynes Bayley or a twentieth-century mystery poem, such as 'Prince Kano' by Edward Lowbury.

Mastermind

Hopefully, most of your students will have seen the programme on television, or at least know about it. If you have a soft-backed teacher's chair (as I did) use it. I have found that students enjoy sitting in the teacher's chair, so any teacher's chair will do. Otherwise, make one of the student chairs different in some way. Perhaps drape a sash over it! Ask for a student volunteer to take the chair and then ask that student twenty questions to do with English. Perhaps as a revision exercise from a book or a play that you have studied, or ask them to (for example) define a semi-colon. You will need five students in total and the one who has the highest number of questions right, is the mastermind.

I allowed students to play this game at least twice a term. With some groups, I allowed them to devise the questions and I sat in the chair . . . mostly the questions centred on a book they had studied. The students learned by finding the right questions to ask and by (hopefully) my answers to their questions.

Literary heritage through drama

Asking students to turn a piece of text they have studied into a play reinforces the learning of that text. They seem to understand what is going on better if **they** can turn it into a play. If you have a large class, split them into groups of four and ask different groups to take a chapter. I usually say something like, 'Group A, take Chapter One, group B take Chapter Two' . . . and so on. You can do this with any age group.

When the groups have turned parts of the book into a play, ask them to read it through and then allow them rehearsal time. They can then put the play together as a class and you can watch the performance. If any vital information is left out, or any group has misunderstood what has gone on, other group members have the right to point this out during a plenary session. You also have the right to point out any inaccuracies.

Possibly the best performance I saw was a Year 13 group reinterpreting *The Mayor of Casterbridge* by Thomas Hardy. They kept to the text, but the fermity tent scene was done by mime and narration. The narration was from Susan's point of view.

There is no reason why your students should not script any book you are studying – from Year 7 to Year 11. It is a good learning technique, in my opinion. The students enjoy doing it, they are working from a structure and they get to know the book better. Try turning part of a Charles Dickens novel into a play. He was well aware of theatre and turned some of his own works into plays. The first scene from *Great Expectations* is a good one for students to turn into a play. Arthur Conan Doyle's *Sherlock Holmes* short stories are also good to turn into plays. Below is a start of a *Sherlock Holmes* short story turned into a play by three students I taught a few years ago. They were Year 9 students. See if you can get hold of the story and photocopy it for your students. They can then complete the play.

'Five Orange Pips' by Arthur Conan Doyle

(adapted as a play by Sanjay Patel, Mia Cushing and Rob Kendrick)
(Sherlock Holmes and Dr Watson are in Holme's quarters at Baker Street. It is a foul night. The wind is howling and the rain is lashing against the window pane. Watson is reading a sea story and Holmes is cross-indexing his records of crimes. The bell rings.)

Dr Watson: *(to Holmes)* Why, that was surely the bell. Who would come tonight? A client?

Holmes: If so, it is a serious case. Nothing less would bring a man out on such a day at such an hour. *(hearing somebody tapping on the door)* Come in!

(A young man entered. He was dripping wet, his face was pale and his eyes heavy, like those of a man who is weighed down with some great anxiety.)

Man: *(taking off his wet coat)* I owe you an apology. I trust I am not intruding. I fear I have brought some traces of the storm and rain into your snug room.

(You will need to get hold of the story. Then ask your students to work in groups of three or four to split the story up and then each group can work with a section of the story to produce a complete play. Alternatively, you can ask them to complete the play and – if you have the story – compare their interpretation with the original.)

Drama approaches to a text

Plays were produced to be acted out. Whatever play you are studying, allow your students to act at least part of it! They can use some of the dramatic techniques mentioned in this book.

Act before you write

I have discovered that some students find difficulty visualizing a story. Ask them to write a creative essay with the title, 'Nightmare House' and some will scribble away, writing pages of interesting prose. Others will not have started. It is much better allocating them into groups of about four and getting them to thought shower ideas. Give them a fifteen-minute time schedule and then ask them to act out the ideas they have thought showered, as an improvisation.

The improvisation should take another fifteen minutes. Bring the class together for a plenary, asking them what worked well and what needed improving. Then ask them to plan their essay (individually) and either complete for homework or complete the next lesson.

I guarantee that the essay outcome would be much better than if you just set them an essay title. Try it!

Drama and Geography

Flooded homes is an area that is on the AQA geography syllabus. Below is an interesting approach that will keep the students focused and interested.

Ask your students to look at areas of Britain (or the world) that have suffered floods or are prone to flooding.

Your students can then research as to why flooding is more prevalent in recent years. Is this due to climatic change or to local authorities/governments allowing the building of new homes on flood planes . . . thus diverting water elsewhere?

To reinforce learning, you could ask your students to split into pairs and imagine Student A is a victim of flooding and Student B is a reporter. They could improvise or write a script as in the brief example below. They have probably watched such interviews on television.

Interviewing a victim of flooding

Reporter: (*stepping over debris from the floods*) So what happened, Mr Griggs?

Mr Griggs: (*upset*) My home was flooded within hours. As you can see – it's a complete mess!

Reporter: Have you lost anyone?

Mr Griggs: (*breathing a sigh of relief*) Thankfully, the cat and my old mother were rescued by boat.

Reporter: Didn't you have any defences?

Mr Griggs: (*shrugs his shoulders*) We were given sand bags the day before the floods. I packed them tightly around my front door . . . but, they proved useless.

Reporter: (*sympathetic*) Looks like you've been left with a mess.

Mr Griggs: (*upset*) It isn't just river water in here. It's sewage . . . the drains overflowed. I only changed the carpets two months ago. I'm not sure the insurance covers all this!

Ask your students to take it in turns to be the reporter and the victim.

By researching the information and scripting a play, your students will have learned a great deal about the subject before you present them with more information. Independent learning and research, in my experience, reinforces learning. Your students should understand the subject better and will remember it for longer!

Flood investigation

In groups of four or five, ask your students to sift through the evidence and carry out an investigation as to what factors are responsible for the flooding. They should appoint a chairperson, a councillor, a government official (or local MP) a weather expert and a resident (victim of flooding).

The group should report their findings back to you in a plenary session.

How does it feel?

In small groups of three or four, your students should take one of the following topics – forest fires, drought or a place at war. Using books from the library, Geography textbooks and the internet, they can investigate one of the above areas. Your students can then record (or write) an interview imagining one of them has lived through a forest fire, a drought or a place at war.

A Geography teacher colleague of mine actually sent some students to interview senior citizens who had lived through disasters, such as a place at war. They used the stories to influence their interviews.

Your students can then show the recording or conduct the interview in front of the class. These ideas enable students to think for themselves. They also gain some prior knowledge of these areas of the subject before you teach them anything.

Drama and Maths
Number games

A) For a lower ability Year 7 or Year 8 group, allocate them into groups of five. If the class is twenty-six or thirty-one, ask them what they can do to make the groups equal. They might come up with the idea that they cannot make equal groups . . . there is one person too many. They might possibly suggest the extra person could be cut into equal parts.

If the class is even, sit one student out! The idea is to help students understand odd and even and how to divide parts until portions are even.

Another possibility is to bring in a large cake and ask students how it can be divided between an odd number of people. I knew a maths teacher who did this with a special needs group. By seeing how odd and even work, the students understood the concept.

B) Ask your group to start counting in unison. When they reach eleven, ask them to quickly take away six and begin counting again at the correct number. When they begin counting from nine, ask them to take away three. Do this until they are eventually able to reach twenty.

As a variation, throw a die (singular) or dice (dice is plural) and whatever number(s) lands upwards, they take that number away.

Sharing

Ask your group to physically divide crayons, pens, pencils into five equal piles. Make sure this cannot be done and allow them to work out that they have to negotiate with each other – so that one group ends up with an extra crayon and the other an extra pen, etc. Tell them beforehand that they cannot break the pens, crayons and pencils!

League tables

I soon discovered in teaching that boys, in particular, are fascinated by football league tables. I admit that my son and I share that fascination! You can make up a league table such as the one below. Or you can use my example, below.

Friday League: Under Fifteens, Football league Table

	Won	Drawn	Lost	Played	Points
Brightwell	5	1	0	6	16
Swilland	4	1	2	7	13
Hazeldene	3	1	1	5	10
Leiston	3	1	1	4	10
Theberton	3	1	2	6	10
Boydon	2	3	1	6	9
Kesgrave	2	1	3	6	7
Claydon	2	1	2	5	7
Ashfield	2	1	3	6	7
Gosbeck	1	0	4	5	3

Show your students the league table (the top ten out of sixteen clubs) and then ask them how the league tables would change after the following results.

Brightwell 6 V Gosbeck 1
Hazeldene 0 V Leiston 0

Claydon 2   V   Swilland 3
Boydon 3   V   Theberton 1
Kesgrave 0   V   Ashford 1

Your students should award three points for a win and one for a draw.

As a variation, for the next football games, your students could use a die to decide the outcome of the games. They can then change the football league tables to include the points won from these games.

Kesgrave V Brightwell
Claydon V Swilland
Gosbeck V Ashford
Theberton V Boydon
Leiston V Hazeldene

For a difficult task, your students could add the other six teams at the bottom of the league and work out the results of the first five games of the following season. They will need to invent the names of six teams. I looked at a map and took villages /towns in Suffolk as my teams.

Looking at the league tables and noticing some teams have played more games than others, can your students work out the **average** number of games played so far? Can they **predict** the likely league top three from the games played so far – and the points won and lost?

They will have noticed that there are several teams on the same amount of points. How are they placed in order? The goal differences count. I have not added these, but students are welcome to do so. They are calculated as following;

For   Against
34   24   = a plus of 10.
For another team, it might be–

For   Against
20   16   = a plus of 4.
The team with a + score of 10 is placed first.

This exercise brings in counting accuracy (adding the wins and draws for the correct points).

Drama and Science
a) What drugs can do
You may use the following information to teach your students about drug awareness or you may prefer to use your own information, or text book information.

Alcohol

Alcohol is mostly absorbed through the stomach and the small intestines. It is a food because it has calories, but does not need to be digested and proceeds directly into the body through the digestive system. After ingestion it is carried through the blood stream and crosses the blood–brain barrier, at which time the brain reacts. A greater amount of ingestion causes greater impairment to the brain; this will cause anyone to have a greater degree of difficulty in functioning.

Alcohol is the most abused drug in our country and people drinking heavily do not realize they are becoming dependent on alcohol. It can cause damage to an unborn baby and it reduces sensitivity to pain. It also affects vision in that it narrows the vision field and reduces resistance to glare. It also lessons sensitivity to colour differentiation. It can cause damage to the liver, the heart and the pancreas. It is linked to high blood pressure and some cancers.

There are certain tests to test if somebody has drunk too much. There are;

a) Blood analysis – by measuring the amount of alcohol per 1,000 drops of blood.
b) Breathalysers – to measure the amount of blood alcohol content of air in the lungs.
c) Urinalysis – which detects the presence of alcohol.

Armed with these facts and any that you may wish to give your students, they should act out a scenario where somebody has been arrested for drink driving. They should be allocated groups of about four.

In groups of four, your students could debate whether alcohol should be banned for certain groups of people. They have learned that alcohol is the most abused drug in the country – what should be done to lessen the use of alcohol? Do they consider alcohol to be a dangerous drug!

Ask your students to suggest practical ways in which they can reduce alcohol abuse.

Your students should write a brief report listing their findings after the debate.

The environment

Tell your students that there is to be a new housing estate on a school playing field. The fields are to be sold off in order that the school will make a profit and divert the money into purchasing new computers. A road will run through the middle of the school, which could be the extension of the motorway.

Ask them what do they think will be the environmental impact.

Ask them to form a meeting in which the local planning officer, the chair of school governors, a parent and the local MP will be present. They must decide who is for and who is against the development. They should then debate the issues.

Use of energy

It is beyond the scope of this book to go through all the factors but your students should imagine that Britain will run out of energy (electricity) in the year 2021 – which is not too far away! What should the Government do? Should they put more money into renewable energy, which some people think will not supply our energy needs, or should they build more power stations very quickly? The Government could extend the 'life' of existing nuclear power stations or buy in power from countries such as France, which will make electricity very expensive.

In groups of four, ask your students to debate the issue and report its findings to you in a plenary session.

Outer space

Ask your students to research information about our solar system and beyond and debate if any of the known planets might sustain life.

Drama and Religious Education

Beliefs and authority

Ask your students to take a story from any religion they have studied and act it out as an improvisation. They should explore how a character felt – for example Moses and the Israelites as they walked through the Red Sea – or the Egyptians as they tried to do the same. It might be possible to use some drama techniques such as blocking in (page 98) or facing out (page 98). Perhaps the main character(s) could be hot seated (page 35) to explore how they felt about the situation they were in.

Social justice

What is right? Allocate your students into groups of four. Ask your students to debate the following;

Is it right in a Christian country for anyone to be homeless? What can be done to help the homeless?

Should we allow people to sell 'The Big Issue' in areas where it is easy to get a job?

Should we allow Euthanasia for people who want to die?

How can young people with families be helped to afford a house of their own?

When your students have completed their debates, ask them to report back their findings in a plenary session.

Global issues

Allocate your students into groups of four. Give your students any necessary information, such as recent disasters, appeals and reviews of appeals and then ask your students to debate the following questions;

What can be done to stop people suffering through wars?

How can famine areas be given food?

How should rich countries react to disasters?

Are religious groups (countries) more likely to respond to helping others than secular groups (countries)?

Drama and History

1) Ask your students to role play any area you have studied. This allows them to 'see' and therefore understand what went on. For example, ask them to act out a poem from the First World War, or a scene between Henry VIII and Catherine of Aragon, when he wanted to divorce her.

I know of one history teacher who actually 'borrowed' the drama room and turned the room into the trenches, so that the students understood something of what it must have been like for those fighting in that particular war.

2) *Medicine.* Ask your class to split into groups of four. They should then choose four people who have contributed to our understanding of medicine. Each member of the group must choose to be one of the four characters and discover as much as they can about their chosen character. They should then imagine these four people from a point in history are in a hot air balloon, which is sinking fast. Only one person can stay in the balloon. Each student must defend why their character should remain in the balloon. The rest of the class must vote!

The object of the exercise is that each member of the class is discovering (or as a revision exercise, rediscovering) about a character who is important to medicine. By defending that character, the rest of the group/class are informed about that person's contribution towards medicine and they learn more about that subject.

As a teacher, you can ask questions to any student in the balloon and add information at the end of the debate.

3) *Elizabethan England*. Allow your students to form into groups of four or five and ask them to debate what they believe were the most important discoveries made during the Elizabethan period of history. Once they have come to a conclusion, they must form a consensus as to what was the single most important discovery. They must then research all they can about that discovery and defend their decision to the rest of the group/class.

4) *The Media in the age of television* Ask your students to form into groups of four or five and ask them to debate if television has had a positive or negative effect on society. For example, do soap operas reflect societies' attitudes or do they influence the way society thinks?

CHAPTER 9

Choosing options, assessment and revision

When students are choosing drama as a GCSE option, they need to bear in mind that they will be expected to work **collaboratively** in groups and that one part of the final examination will be assessed by an external examiner. They also need to consider the act that marks are given to performances and their practical ability will be assessed.

For revision, ask your students to define the following; Parallel cross-cutting, rhythm (relating to drama), noise collage and contrasts. If they have forgotten, direct them to the relevant page. The relevant pages are 39, 62, 99 and 64.

Ask them to write the first page of a radio play. They must set out the script correctly.

Summing it up

The Edexcel exam group expects GCSE students to know the following – still image, thought tracking, narrating , hot seating, role play, cross-cutting, forum theatre, the use of masks/make-up, the use of sound and music, lighting, space and levels, sets and props, mime and gesture. Also, the use of voice and use of the spoken language. All these aspects of drama are covered in this book.

Appendix:
exam board specification/websites

Edexcel at www.edexcel.com/quals/gcse/gcse09/drama
Edexcel states the following;

- The course encourages students to work imaginatively and creatively in a collaborative context, creating, developing and communicating ideas.
- The specification has a clear, three-unit structure. Two units assessed by the teacher and a third assessed by an external examiner.
- Free choice stimulus material.
- Final exam performance-based rather than written. Marks given to performance and practical ability.

The AQA GCSE Drama examination is split into three sections.

A: Is a practical work that students need to complete during the course.

B: Involves the study and performance of a scripted play.

C: Is the study of a live theatre production that students have seen.

Web:aqa.org.uk/qual/newgcses/drama

WJEC

The WJEC specification fosters candidates' creativity, personal growth, self-confidence, communication and analytical skills through the acquisition of knowledge, skills and understanding and the exercise of the imagination. It also promotes students' involvement in and enjoyment of drama as performers, devisers, directors and designers. It provides opportunities for students to attend professional and community dramatic performances and to develop their skills as informed and thoughtful audience members. Through the study of this specification, students will be given opportunities to participate in and interpret their own and others' drama. They will investigate the forms, styles and contexts of drama and will learn to work collaboratively to develop ideas, to express feelings, to experiment with technical elements and to reflect on their own and others' performances.

www.wjec.co.uk

Whichever exam board you decide to follow, your students will be fulfilled in what appears to be an exciting two-year study.

References

Advice from Childline – www. childline.org.uk

'Back To The Future' One (1985) Two (1989), Three (1990) films directed by Zemeekis, R.

Brothers Grimm (1890) 'The Twelve Brothers' From 'The Red Fairy Book'. Smith and Elder.

Conan-Doyle, A. (1891) 'Five Orange Pips' The Strand Magazine.

Cottrell Boyce, F. (2004) 'Millions' Macmillan.

Dickens, C. (1850) 'David Copperfield' Bradbury and Evans.

Dickens, C. (1860–1861) 'Great Expectations'. All Year Round.

'Fireproof'(2008) film directed by Kendrick A.

Golding, W. (1954) 'Lord of the Flies'. Faber and Faber.

Gould, M. (2004) 'Page to Stage' Heinemann.

Hardy, T. (1886) 'The Mayor of Casterbridge' The Literary Magazine, 'Graphic.'

'Inception' (2010) film directed by Christopher Nolan.

'Lost' T. V. Series. Abrams, J. J., Leiber, J., Lindelof, D.

Macphail C (2001) 'Tribes' Puffin.

O'Connor, J. (2001) 'Scripts and Sketches' Heinemann.

Priestly, J. B. (1945) 'An Inspector Calls'. Heinemann.

'Punch and Judy' (1851) London Labour and London Poor.

Shakespeare, W. (1951) 'Hamlet' The Alexander Text, Collins.

Shakespeare, W. (1951) 'Henry IV Part Two' The Alexander Text, Collins.

Shakespeare, W. (1951) 'Macbeth' The Alexander Text, Collins.

Shakespeare, W. (1951) 'Othello' The Alexander Text, Collins.

Shakespeare, W. (1951) 'Romeo and Juliet' The Alexander Text, Collins.

Shakespeare, W. (1951) 'The Tempest' The Alexander Text, Collins.

Vaughan, H. (1650) 'The World'.

West, K. (1990) 'The Big Match' Rigg Publications.

West, K. (2001) 'Jason Brent' Evans Brothers.

West, K. (2010) 'Inspired English Teaching' Continuum.

Williams, T. (2001) 'Cat On A Hot Tin Roof' Penguin Classics.

Index